Collins

Revised Edition

EXCURSIONS

Geography

7

Author
Sukanya Chakraborty

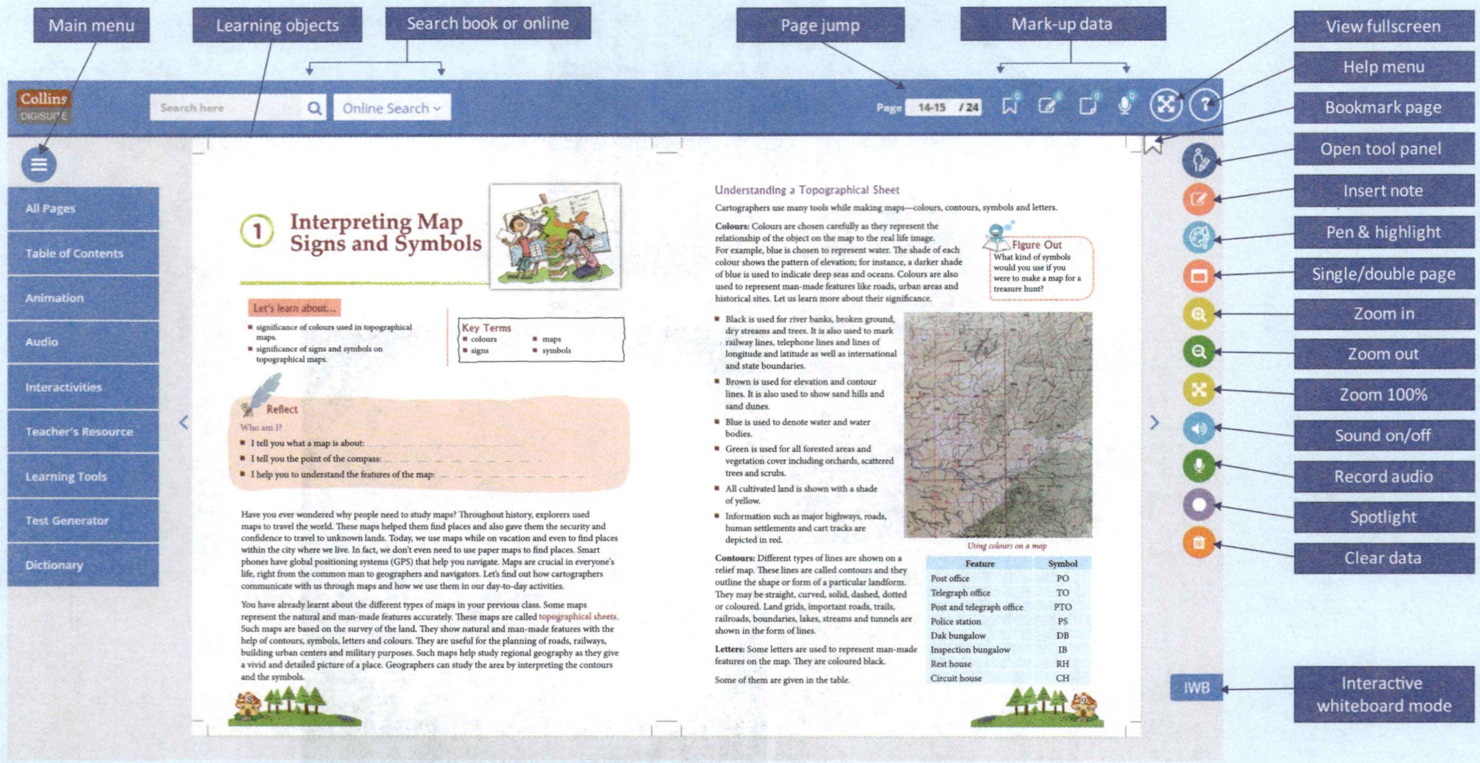

Student + Teacher		Teacher-only
a animations	**ia** activities	**lp** lesson plans
ilt instructor-led tutorials	**w** worksheets	**w** worksheets
	audio	**tn** teacher's notes
g games	**v** videos	**ak** answer keys

Preface

'Education is not the learning of facts, but the training of the mind to think.'

Albert Einstein

Excursions Revised Edition is a comprehensive course in Environmental Studies and Social Studies for young learners. This series for classes 1 to 8 has been aligned with the guidelines given in the National Education Policy, 2020. Following the curriculum, *Excursions* Revised Edition offers a course in Environmental Studies for classes 1 and 2, integrated Social Studies course for classes 3, 4 and 5 and separate Geography and History and Civics courses for classes 6, 7 and 8. The series offers features that focus on essential skills to assist learners achieve holistic learning through a multidisciplinary approach.

Each book in the series is divided into a number of themes that help students connect directly to the environment. Each theme follows a branch of geography. Practical geography deals with representation of geographical features through cartography. Physical geography focuses on understanding the Earth, its flora and fauna and atmosphere. Human and economic geography deals with the patterns and processes that shape the human society. Lastly, Regional geography addresses the unique geographical characteristics of a particular place.

This series carefully combines aspects of physical and social science as geography involves the study of the physical, biological and sociocultural environment and their relationship with human life. *Excursions* Revised Edition also provides an opportunity to the students to understand multidisciplinary links and connect their knowledge of geography to other subjects. A number of teaching methods such as case studies, application-based activities and research-based project work reinforces the concepts learnt.

About the author

Sukanya Chakraborty is a self-motivated educator with more than twenty years of experience in teaching. A Fulbright TEA fellow, she has worked at Bhavan's Nandvidya Niketan and ESSAR International School. She has planned and presented a wide range of lessons to meet the needs of various abilities and age levels. An avid geographer, Sukanya actively conducts workshops around the country.

Key Features

Varied key features in the series hone learning skills.

- **Learning** – Let's learn about, Key terms, Timeline, In a Nutshell
- **Extended learning and explanation** – Reflect, FactPedia, Figure Out, Weblinks
- **Observation and application** – DIY, Green Earth, World Connect, Geo Connect, Case Study
- **Problem-solving and analytical thinking** – Think Box, Life Skills and Values, Picture Study
- **Creativity and happiness** – Enjoy, Game
- **Multidisciplinary and holistic learning** – Across the Boundary, Snap Recap
- **Assessment and practice** – Workout, Test Yourself, Outline maps

The comprehensive teacher's resource materials are aimed at facilitating teaching and assessment. Feedback and suggestions to improve the course further are welcomed.

Key Features

Excursions Revised Edition offers features that focus on essential skills to assist learners achieve holistic learning through a multidisciplinary approach. In so doing, the series is aligned with the guidelines given in the National Education Policy, 2020.

Learning

Let's learn about...

- a globe and its uses.
- a map and its uses.
- sketch and plans.

Outlines the learning outcomes of the chapter

Key Terms

- map
- scale
- sign
- grid
- globe
- key
- colours
- plan
- Earth
- symbol
- sketch

Lists the important terms used in the chapter

In a Nutshell

- South America lies totally in the Western Hemisphere. A larger part of it falls in the Southern Hemisphere.

Gives a ready reckoner to reinforce learning

Extended Learning and Application

Reflect

How have each of these innovations influenced history?

Includes warm-up tasks to initiate the learners into the topic and relate to it

FactPedia

The symbols and letters used by the Survey of India are set out in a sheet called the characteristic sheet.

Provides interesting titbits of information

Figure Out

What type of drainage patterns does your town have?

Hones referencing and research skills through small tasks

Weblinks

For more information, visit
http://mocomi.com/landforms/
Last accessed on 31/July/2020

Encourages the use of technology for extended learning

Observation and Application

Green Earth

Is ivory trade still permitted today? How does it harm nature?

Sensitizes learners towards conservation of the environment

Geo Connect

Technology has continually changed in order to meet the demands of new generations of cartographers and map users. While scientists

Helps students compare the developments of one region in relation to other parts of the world

DIY

Identify three centres of the Indus Valley Civilization in the map given below.

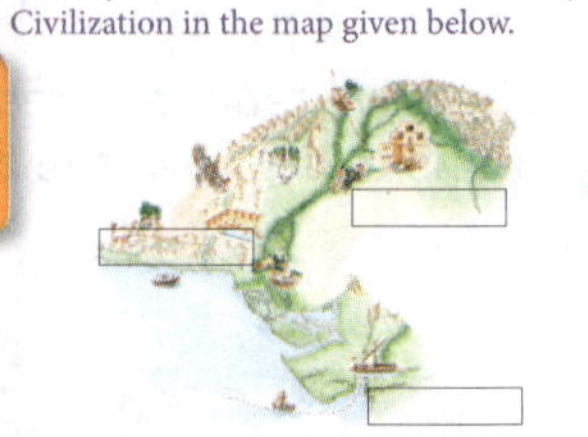

Provides application-based activities for experiential learning

Problem-solving and Analytical Tasks

Think Box

Unscramble the letters to find out the names associated with South America.

ELSSVA	....	ROOCOIN	....
XPACITOO	....	MAATCAA	....
GYRAPAUA	....	ZAONAM	....
DSEAN	....	LIBZAR	....
MAAPSP	....		

(HOTS) Facilitates out-of-the-box thinking for curious minds

Picture Study

Look at the picture and answer these questions.

1. What can you infer about the Mughal period from this painting?

Provides exercises for inferential learning

Creativity and Happiness

Enjoy

Take a print out of a world map and cut out the continents. Join their boundaries and paste them on another sheet of paper. Take a map of Pangaea and compare it to the map you created using the different continents.

Addresses wellbeing and happiness of the students through creative and fun tasks

Multidisciplinary and Holistic Learning

Across the Boundary 2

Be a Journalist

Agriculture is important as it provides food to us. We depend on farmers for this basic requirement. Do you know that the life of Indian farmers is very difficult as they work day in and day out. Imagine you are a journalist and interview a farmer based on the following issues:

- Daily work and type of crops grown in the field
- Financial management and difficulties faced
- Importance of education for farmers
- Importance of health and hygiene

Based on the information gathered, write a short report covering these points:

- The dependence of farmers on the monsoon and the difficulties
- Problems ...

Provides varied activities for multidisciplinary learning

Snap Recap

The Snap Recap section contains a collection of mind maps that draw the outline of the concepts that you have learned in this book. Mind mapping is a useful technique that helps you learn more effectively and improves the way that you record information. They help you see the way pieces of information fit together. Mind maps also help you remember information, as they hold it in a format that your mind finds easy to recall.

Major landforms of the Earth

- Mountains
  - Fold
- Plateaus
  - Tectonic
- Plains

Provides mind maps for quick learning

Assessment and Practice

Workout

A. Choose the correct option and fill in the blanks.

1. Egypt is situated on the banks of the river ....

To facilitate assessment

TEST YOURSELF I

Maximum marks: 50

A. Fill in the blanks. ½×20=10

1. .... is a three-dimensional model of the Earth.
2. A detailed drawing of a small area is known as ....
3. The .... maps show a large area in a small size.
4. The science of map making is called ....
5. Rift valleys are also known as ....
6. Plains formed at the foot of the mountains are called ....
7. A shallow sea that is completely enclosed by land is called a ....
8. .... is the world's warmest ocean.
9. Plateaus are storehouse of ....
10. .... fold mountains have a lower altitude.
11. America was discovered by ....

To facilitate evaluation

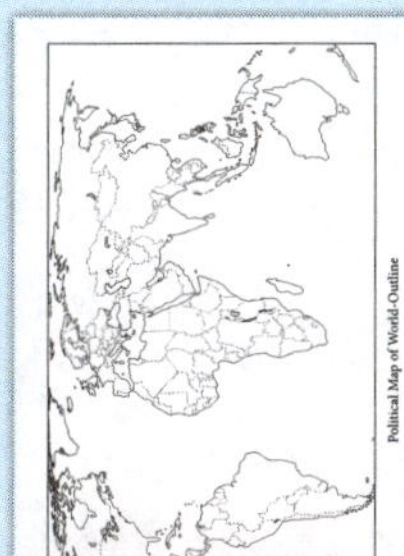

Imparts map skill practice

Contents

Theme 1

Representation of Geographical Features

Studying maps is an important part of geography. Maps convey a considerable amount of information in a limited space. The ability to read maps and understand the information given in a limited space needs expertise. Maps give information by using symbols and colours. A good map aims to maintain a balance between the text, symbols and the detailed information. Thus, the knowledge and judgment of a cartographer plays an important role in map-making.

In the following chapters, you will study about the different symbols and colours used by cartographers to represent information in the maps. A map represents a region accurately. To make maps accurate, cartographers draw maps on a scale which they express as a ratio between the distance on the map to the actual distance on the ground. There are many ways by which they express the scale which we will study in the following chapters. A map is an essential part of communication. More recently, a geographic information system (GIS) has revolutionized the mapping of a region. Maps are actually graphical representations of the Earth and its features. Each map needs to have a relation between the features of the Earth and what is represented on the map.

1 Interpreting Map Signs and Symbols

Let's learn about...

- significance of colours used in topographical maps.
- significance of signs and symbols on topographical maps.

Key Terms

- colours
- maps
- signs
- symbols

Reflect

Who am I?

- I tell you what a map is about: ....
- I tell you the point of the compass: ....
- I help you to understand the features of the map: ....

Have you ever wondered why people need to study maps? Throughout history, explorers used maps to travel the world. These maps helped them find places and also gave them the security and confidence to travel to unknown lands. Today, we use maps while on vacation and even to find places within the city where we live. In fact, we don't even need to use paper maps to find places. Smart phones have global positioning systems (GPS) that help you navigate. Maps are crucial in everyone's life, right from the common man to geographers and navigators. Let's find out how cartographers communicate with us through maps and how we use them in our day-to-day activities.

You have already learnt about the different types of maps in your previous class. Some maps represent the natural and man-made features accurately. These maps are called topographical sheets. Such maps are based on the survey of the land. They show natural and man-made features with the help of contours, symbols, letters and colours. They are useful for the planning of roads, railways, building urban centers and military purposes. Such maps help study regional geography as they give a vivid and detailed picture of a place. Geographers can study the area by interpreting the contours and the symbols.

Understanding a Topographical Sheet

Cartographers use many tools while making maps—colours, contours, symbols and letters.

Colours: Colours are chosen carefully as they represent the relationship of the object on the map to the real life image. For example, blue is chosen to represent water. The shade of each colour shows the pattern of elevation; for instance, a darker shade of blue is used to indicate deep seas and oceans. Colours are also used to represent man-made features like roads, urban areas and historical sites. Let us learn more about their significance.

> **Figure Out**
> What kind of symbols would you use if you were to make a map for a treasure hunt?

- Black is used for river banks, broken ground, dry streams and trees. It is also used to mark railway lines, telephone lines and lines of longitude and latitude as well as international and state boundaries.
- Brown is used for elevation and contour lines. It is also used to show sand hills and sand dunes.
- Blue is used to denote water and water bodies.
- Green is used for all forested areas and vegetation cover including orchards, scattered trees and scrubs.
- All cultivated land is shown with a shade of yellow.
- Information such as major highways, roads, human settlements and cart tracks are depicted in red.

Using colours on a map

Contours: Different types of lines are shown on a relief map. These lines are called contours and they outline the shape or form of a particular landform. They may be straight, curved, solid, dashed, dotted or coloured. Land grids, important roads, trails, railroads, boundaries, lakes, streams and tunnels are shown in the form of lines.

Letters: Some letters are used to represent man-made features on the map. They are coloured black.

Some of them are given in the table.

Feature	Symbol
Post office	PO
Telegraph office	TO
Post and telegraph office	PTO
Police station	PS
Dak bungalow	DB
Inspection bungalow	IB
Rest house	RH
Circuit house	CH

Conventional signs and symbols: We use conventional signs and symbols to represent man-made and natural features on a map. These symbols help cartographers give detailed information on a small surface. The colours along with the symbols are used so that readers do not get confused. Most of the signs and symbols are standardized and used throughout the world. Every map has a legend or a key. The list of signs and symbols along with their meanings is given which give us information about the geographical features depicted in the map.

> **FactPedia**
> The symbols and letters used by the Survey of India are set out in a sheet called the characteristic sheet.

Let us explore the important symbols according to colours used in a topographical map.

Blue		
Waterbody	**Conventional symbol**	**Geographical interpretation**
Stream		A small stream of running water also called *nala*
River		A natural flow of water larger than stream, also called *nadi*
Riverbed (dry)	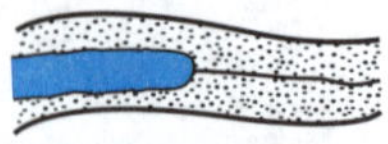	Seasonal rivers which almost dry up in summer in semi-arid regions
River with rocks and islands	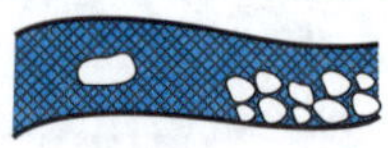	Rivers that start depositing as they move towards their lower course forming islands
Unlined well		A well without any brick or stone lining
Lined well		A well with stones and bricks; it is a perennial source of water
Tube well		A deep bore dug into the Earth's surface to extract groundwater with the help of a pump; its presence indicates agricultural land

Green		
Vegetation	**Conventional symbol**	**Geographical interpretation**
Grass		Found in regions where rainfall is not sufficient to support trees
Open scrub		A type of grassland which indicates semi-desert region with scanty rainfall
Swamp	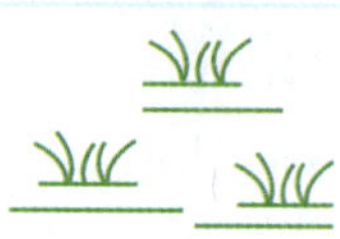	Found along coastal areas and around lakes and rivers; it is permanently covered with stagnant water and water weeds
Reserved forest	RF	An area where cutting of trees are not legally allowed
Protected forest	PF	Known as shelter belts, they protect the land from erosion

Black		
Feature	**Conventional symbol**	**Geographical interpretation**
International boundaries		Boundaries for different countries
State boundaries		They demarcate two or more states within a country
District boundaries		Borders within a state
Broad Gauge Railway		When the distance between two rails is 1.69 m, it is known as broad gauge. It carries both passengers and goods.
Railway line with station		Areas near human settlements where trains halt or stop for boarding and de-boarding

Red		
Feature	**Conventional symbol**	**Geographical interpretation**
Metaled road (pukka roads)		Metaled roads found in developed regions
Metaled roads with milestones	20	Metaled roads shown with stones to indicate distance in kilometers
Un-metaled roads		Also known as kutcha roads, they indicate that the region is undeveloped
Cart track		Paths used by bullocks or horse carts found in rural areas
Pack tracks		Pathways made by humans and animals due to prolonged travel
Foot path		Mainly found in the steep regions
Dam		A man-made structure across the river to utilize the river water for irrigation and also to control flood
Dispersed settlements	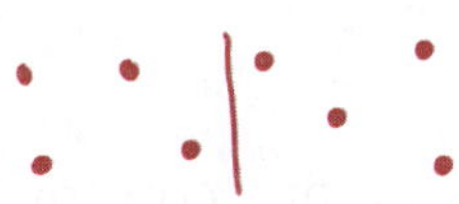	Found in highland areas that have sparse population
Linear settlements	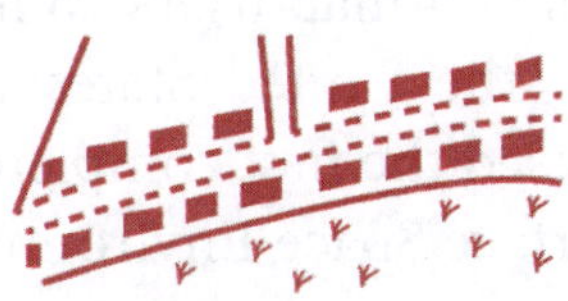	Found along river banks and roads, these settlements usually stretch like a ribbon. They are mainly trade and commerce centers.

Fort	Temple	Church	Mosque	Tomb	Light House

DIY

Find out the symbols given by the Survey of India for the following features and draw them in the space provided.

Feature	Conventional symbol	Geographical interpretation
Waterfall		Formed when the water falls from a great height in hilly regions
Confluence		The intersecting point where a tributary comes and joins the main river
Tank		Perennial tanks found in hilly regions that have water throughout; also known as *talao*
Deciduous forest		The most widespread natural vegetation in India
Scattered vegetation		Trees and scrubs, widely spaced, indicating that the region has moderate or scanty rainfall.
Narrow gauge railway		The distance between the rails is 0.77m. These are light railways and carry only passengers.
Level crossing		Places where the road crosses one or more railway lines
Railway line with bridge		Bridges are found where land is interrupted by obstacles like lakes, valleys, ponds and rivers
Nucleated settlements		Consists of houses that form compact and concentrated settlements; mainly found in the thickly populated areas in fertile plains
Tunnel		A passage for road or railways through a hill

Geo Connect

Cartography has developed with technology. Technology has continually changed in order to meet the demands of new generations of mapmakers and map users. While scientists have long developed complete topographic maps of the Earth, the United States Geologic Survey, along with some prominent research institutions, have released the first complete topographical map of Mercury. The map is courtesy of NASA's Mercury Surface Space Environment Geochemistry and

Ranging (MESSENGER), the first spacecraft to ever orbit Mercury. MESSENGER was launched in 2004, and has orbited the planet 4,104 times, stitching together more than 1,00,000 images to form the final complete picture.

In a Nutshell

- Legend and key explain each symbol and colour used in the map.
- Colours and symbols are also used to represent man-made and natural features on topographical maps. These symbols are known as conventional signs and symbols.
- Colours and symbols are used to represent many geographical features in a small pace.

Workout

A. Fill in the blanks.

1. Black is used to represent ...., ... and .... on maps.
2. Information such as major highways, roads, human settlements and cart tracks are depicted in ....
3. Cultivated land is represented by the colour ....
4. .... outline the shape or form of a particular landform.

B. Identify these signs and symbols.

....

....

....

....

PO
....

....

....

C. Define the following.

1. characteristic sheet
2. conventional signs and symbols
3. legend
4. contour

D. Answer these questions in brief.

1. Why do we need maps?
2. Which colour is used to denote the following on a topographical map?
   a. elevation information
   b. post office
   c. scrubs
   d. lined wells
   e. human settlement
   f. broken ground
3. Who prepares the topographical maps in India?

4. Differentiate between:
   a. lined well and unlined well
   b. reservoir and tank
   c. broad gauge and meter gauge
   d. reserved forest and protected forest
5. Where do you find the following features?
   a. open scrub
   b. swamp
   c. foot path
   d. level crossing

Think Box

The whole world is connected through satellites. Explore the world using Google Earth and find out how satellite maps help us in locating places.

Picture Study

Look at the picture and answer the questions.

1. Would you say this is a new map or an old map?
2. Is it a correct map of the Earth?
3. What are the differences that you see between this map and the one in your atlas?

Life Skills and Values

Signs and symbols are important for reading maps. Think about the important signs and symbols in our day-to-day life such as symbols used for road safety.

Enjoy

Make a map of your school to plan out the emergency exit in case of any calamity or an accident. Use symbols and make a legend for the map.

Weblinks

For more information, visit
https://www.nationalgeographic.org/education/map-skills-elementary-students/
Last accessed on 31/July/2020

2 Interpreting Map Scales and Distances

Let's learn about...

- types of map scales.
- conversion of map scales.
- types of maps.

Key Terms

- maps
- scales
- conversion
- large-scale maps
- small-scale maps

Reflect

I represent the Earth on a flat surface. I state the location of different places, natural features and give a lot of information about an area. Who am I?

....

We have learnt that a map is a representation of the Earth and its features on a flat surface. How do cartographers represent the Earth, which is round, on a flat surface? Cartographers reduce the representation of the Earth or a specific region. The extent of this reduction is referred to as scale in geography.

Map Scales

Scale is expressed as a ratio of the distance on the map to the actual distance on the ground. Thus, scale is the ratio between a distance measured on a map and the corresponding distance on the Earth.

Verbal or statement scale

A verbal scale helps map readers to understand the scale reduction in terms of units they can more easily imagine. This scale is stated in statements or words. Verbal scales are often used on large-scale maps. It is usually written on a map as 1 cm to 1 km or as 1 inch to 1 mile. The unit of measurement may vary from map to map. The left hand side of the scale indicates the unit of measurement on the map and the right hand side indicates the unit of measurement on the ground. When a map shows that the scale of the map is one centimetre to one kilometre, it means that if you measure one centimetre as a distance between two places on the map, then this would be one kilometre on the surface of the Earth.

Representative fraction scale (RF)

The representative fraction scale is the most common way to present scale on maps. It is also known as a numerical fraction scale. It describes the scale as a simple ratio. A representative fraction is a ratio and is shown as 1:50000. This RF scale means that 1 unit on the map represents 50000 of the same units on the Earth's surface. In the representative fraction scale, the first term of the ratio is always 1. It represents the distance on the map in any unit. The second term of the ratio represents the distance on the Earth's surface. It must be expressed in the same unit of measurement as the first term of the ratio. Let us see how it is presented on a map. If the unit of measurement on the map is 1 cm, the unit of the corresponding distance on the ground will also be in centimetres. Suppose the scale of the map indicates RF is 1/100, it means that any length on the map represents 100 times that length on the ground. This is the most common method to present scale as no unit of measurement is mentioned.

Linear or graphic scale

A linear or a graphic scale is also called a bar scale or a scale bar. It visually shows the relationship between distances on the map and the surface of the Earth. A linear scale is represented as a line marked at intervals to show the distance on the Earth. It is usually divided and subdivided into lengths. Each of these represents a certain distance on the ground. You might have seen a small ruler drawn at the bottom of the map. Observe the ruler carefully. You will see that it is divided and subdivided into lengths. Each of these lengths represents a certain distance on the ground. This graphical scale has a primary and secondary division.

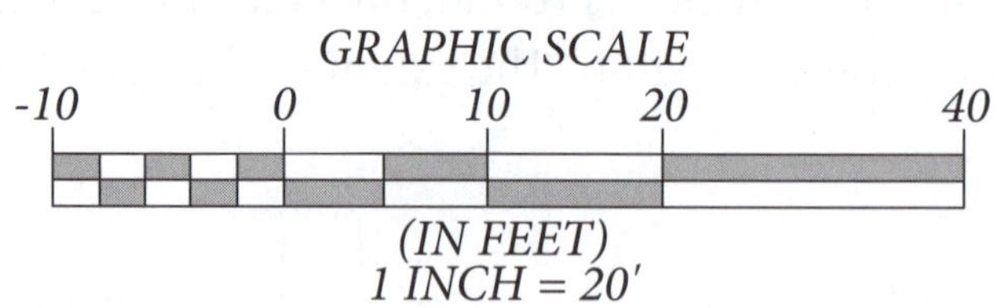

Bar Scale

Scale Conversion

The RF scale is practical because it can be used by everyone. However, it is not very useful when we want to indicate an actual distance between two places. For example, if the RF scale is 1:50,000, then we know that one centimetre on the map represents 50,000 centimetres on the Earth's surface. However, this does not tell us how many kilometres on the Earth's surface are represented by one centimetre on the map. For this reason, it is important that we know how to convert from one scale to another.

Conversion of verbal statement to representative fraction

1. Convert 100 cm to 1 km into representative fractions.

Step 1: Convert km to cm

1 km = 1,00,000 cm

Step 2:
$$\text{R.F} = \frac{\text{map distance in cm}}{\text{ground distance in cm}}$$
$$= \frac{100 \text{ cm}}{1{,}00{,}000\text{cm}} = \frac{1}{1000}$$

therefore, R. F = 1:1000

2. Convert 8 cm to 2 km into representative fraction

Step 1: Convert km to cm

2 km = 2,00,000 cm

Step 2:
$$\text{R.F} = \frac{\text{map distance in cm}}{\text{ground distance in cm}}$$
$$= \frac{8 \text{ cm}}{2{,}00{,}000 \text{ cm}} = \frac{1}{25000}$$

therefore, R.F = 1:25000

3. Convert 1.5 cm to 3 km into representative fraction

Step 1: Convert km to cm

3 km = 3,00,000cm

Step 2:
$$\text{R.F} = \frac{\text{map distance in cm}}{\text{ground distance in cm}}$$
$$= \frac{1.5 \text{ cm}}{3{,}00{,}000 \text{ cm}} = \frac{1}{200000}$$

therefore, R. F = 1:200000

4. Convert 20 cm to 4.5 km into representative fraction

Step 1: Convert km to cm

4.5 km = 4,50,000 cm

Step 2:
$$\text{R.F} = \frac{\text{map distance in cm}}{\text{ground distance in cm}}$$
$$= \frac{20 \text{ cm}}{450000\text{cm}} = \frac{1}{22500}$$

therefore, R.F = 1:22500

Figure Out

Why is a compass a very important instrument for travellers?

Conversion of representative fraction into verbal statement

1. Express 1:20,000 as a verbal statement

Step 1: The scale is 1 cm = 20,000 cm

Step 2: Conversion of cm to km

$$1 \text{ cm} = \frac{1}{100000} \text{ km}$$

$$20{,}000 \text{ cm} = \frac{20000}{100000} = \frac{2}{10} = \frac{1}{5} = 0.2 \text{ km}$$

therefore, the scale is 1 cm to 0.2 km or 5 cm to 1 km.

2. Express 1:25000 as a verbal statement

Step 1: The scale is 1 cm = 25000 cm

Step 2: Conversion of km to cm

$$1 \text{ cm} = \frac{1}{100000} \text{ km}$$

$$25{,}000\text{cm} = \frac{25000}{100000} = \frac{25}{100} = \frac{1}{4} = 0.25 \text{ km}$$

therefore, the scale is 1 cm to 0.25 km or 4 cm to 1 km

3. Express 1:43000 as a verbal statement

Step 1: The scale is 1 cm = 43,000 cm

Step 2: Conversion of cm to km

$$1 \text{ cm} = \frac{1}{100000} \text{ km}$$

$$43{,}000\text{cm} = \frac{43000}{100000} = \frac{43}{100} = 0.43 \text{ km}$$

therefore, the scale is 1 cm to 0.43 km

Remember

To convert centimetres into kilometres, divide the measure by 1,00,000 because 1 km is equal to 1,00,000 cm.

To convert centimetres to metres, divide the measure by 100 because 1 m is equal to 100 cm.

Large-scale and small-scale maps

A map which depicts a small territory is called a large scale map. Cadastral and topographical maps are examples of large scale maps. A large scale map only shows a small area, but it shows it in great detail. A map depicting a large area, such as an entire country, is called a small-scale map. Wallmaps and atlas maps are examples of small scale maps. A small-scale map shows more territory, but it is less detailed. Let us take an example of the river Ganga. On a small-scale map, the Ganga will be shown as a line but in a large-scale map, you will be able to see how the river is meandering, its delta formation and other details.

A large-scale map has a relatively small ratio between the distance on the map and the actual distance on the ground. A map with a scale of 1:10,000 will be a good example. When a unit on the map represents a large area of unit on the ground, for example, 1: 5,000,000, the map is a small-scale map. The R.F. of a large-scale map is relatively larger and the R.F. of a small-scale map is relatively smaller.

FactPedia

An opisometer is an instrument used to measure distances on a map. It is a small instrument which has a milled wheel that can run along a road or a river. The distance covered is indicated on the dial.

On a small-scale map, man-made features such as dams, tunnels and bridges are not shown.

Measuring Distances

Maps are not just useful in determining directions; they can also help us determine the distance between two or more places.

Straight-line distances

A straight-line distance can be measured by placing the straight edge of a strip of paper along the required line. The limits on the strip are marked and then placed along the graphical scale. Alternatively, a divider can be used to measure a straight-line distance on a map.

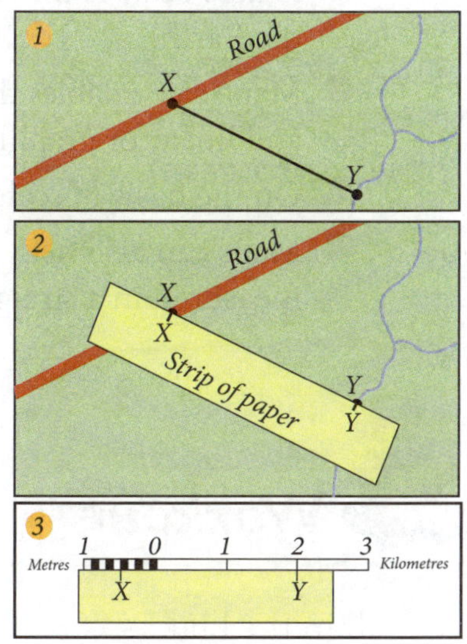

Straight-lined distances

To measure straight-line distances on a map:

- Connect two points on the map that need to be measured.
- Use a strip of paper to mark out the distance between the points.
- Place the strip of paper on the line scale.
- Convert the map distance into actual distance.

Curved-line distances

Curved-line distances are geographical features such as a meandering river or a winding road. These can be measured with the help of a string or a strip of paper.

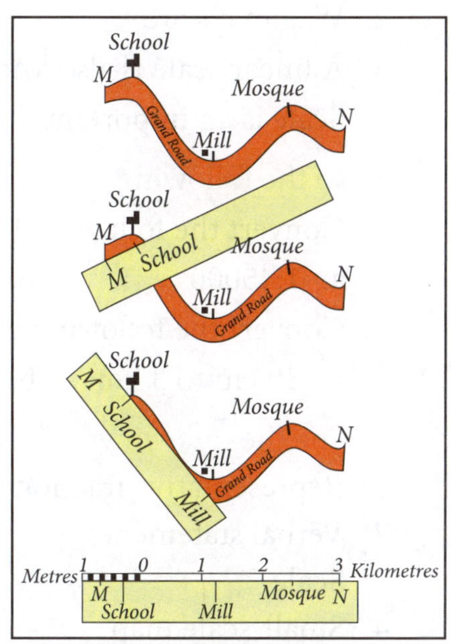

Curved-line distances

To measure curved-line distances using a string:

- Use a string to trace the curved distance.
- Convert it into actual distance using the scale.

To measure curved-line distances using a strip of paper:

- Divide the curved distance into various straight line segments.
- Mark each location on a strip of paper until the whole length of the curved route is marked.
- Place the strip of paper against the scale to convert it into the actual distance.

DIY

On a map of India, draw a triangular route from one city to two other cities and back again to where you started. Measure the kilometres you would travel for each leg of the trip and mark them on the triangle. Add the distances to find out your total miles.

Three cities: ...., ... and ....

Total miles to travel to all three cities and back to the start: ....

In a Nutshell

- A map scale is the relationship between distance on the map and distance on the surface of the Earth.
- Map scale enables the reader to measure distances. Verbal scale, representative fraction scale and linear or graphic scale are types of scales.
- On the basis of scale, there are two types of maps—large-scale maps and small-scale maps.
- Maps can also help us determine the distance between two or more places. Distance can be measured in a straight line as well as curved line using different methods.

Workout

A. Fill in the blanks.

1. Toposheets are .... scale maps.
2. Wall maps are .... scale maps.
3. A linear scale is also known as ....
4. Scale is an important .... of a map

B. Solve the following.

1. Convert the following R.F into verbal statement:

   a. 1:45000 b. 1:50000 c. 1:40000 d. 1:25000

2. Convert the following verbal statement into R.F:

   a. 30 cm to 3 km b. 200 cm to 5 km c. 100 cm to 5 km d. 230 cm to 23 km

C. Define the following.

1. Representative fraction
2. Verbal statement
3. Scale
4. Small-scale map
5. Opisometer

D. Answer these questions in brief.

1. How can you represent scales on a map?
2. Differentiate between:
   a. large-scale maps and small-scale maps
   b. linear scale and verbal statement
3. How would you determine the distance between two places with the help of an opisometer?

Think Box

Topographical maps are becoming obsolete and satellite images are replacing them. The data for these satellite images is collected by remote sensors. These sensors detect the energy that is reflected from the Earth. Find out the names of the devices that work on the remote sensing technology.

Picture Study

Look at the picture and answer the question.

Q. If you were making a map using the symbols given here. What would you represent using each of these symbols?

Life Skills and Values

Mapping the Earth is a very difficult task. Maps tell us a lot about the way people live. Compare maps of your area with another. Discuss your findings with your classmates.

Enjoy

Make a PowerPoint presentation on the history of map-making. Include the modern methods of world mapping in your presentation.

Weblinks

For more information, visit
https://www.nationalgeographic.org/activity/measuring-distances-map/
Last accessed on 31/July/2020

Across the Boundary 1

Be A Cartographer

Read the instructions and complete this activity.

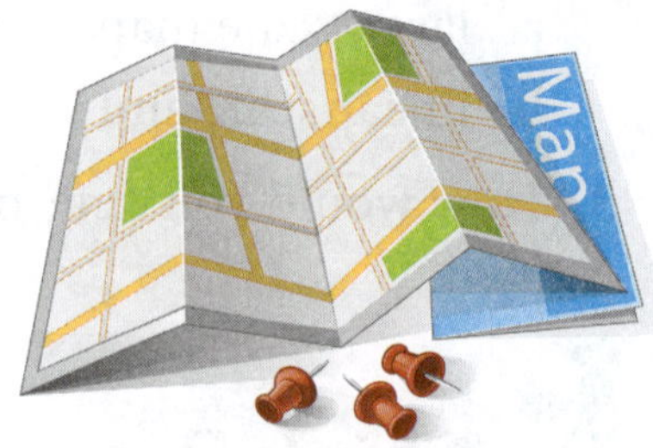

You need to draw a map of Place A. You can first prepare a rough outline of the area. Use conventional symbols and various colours to represent the features of the place. Make a legend and write a title for your map. You can also choose to rename this region.

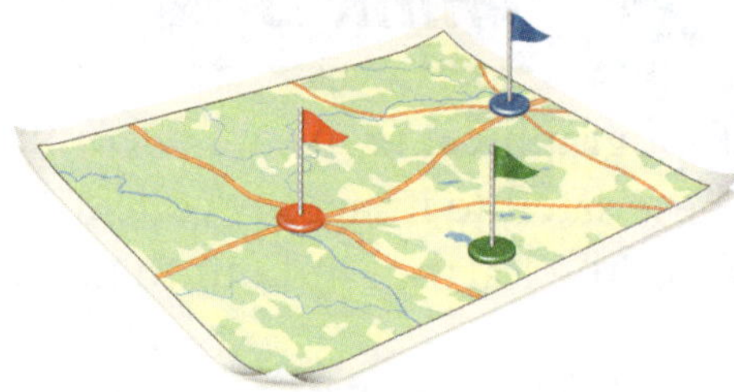

The following are the geographical features of Place A.

1. Towards the northwest of Place A, there is a river that flows towards the southern direction and empties itself into a lake located on its southwestern border. The river flows from north to south.

2. On the eastern part of the river is a nucleated settlement that has a church on the west, a post office on the east, a *dak* bungalow next to the post office and a police station at the centre of the settlement.

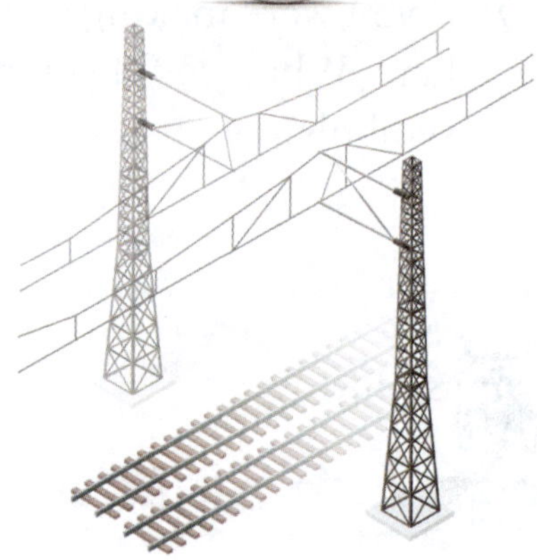

3. A railway track emerges from the nucleated settlement and stretches in a straight-line path towards the west. The railway track extends over a river on a bridge.
4. Towards the north, there is a wide grassland. On the southeastern corner is a deciduous forest. A swamp is near the southern lake where the aforementioned river drains.
5. A metalled road runs parallel to the railway track on the right hand side emerging from the settlement.

6. On the northwest, is a farmland. The region is dotted with four perennial lined wells and a reservoir.

Note:

- The map should have all the necessary elements. Mention whether it is a small-scale or a large-scale map.
- Take the help of your geography teacher to draw the map.
- Determine a suitable scale for your map and calculate the total area under your map with the help of your Maths teacher.
- Take the help of your art and craft teacher to add aesthetic value to you map.

Theme 2

Physical Geography

Geography is a subject that overlaps with many aspects of land, climate, soil and human relationship with nature. Physical geography is mostly concerned about the topography and climate of a region. The study of landforms, their formation and their relationship with people is an important part of physical geography. No geographical study can be complete without an understanding of weather and climate. The climatic elements have a great influence on plant life, animal life and even soil and rocks found in a region. These in turn influence human activity as human beings are dependent on their environment. In the following chapters, you will study how the atmosphere sustains life, how the soil helps plants to grow and how the climate influences our lifestyle.

3 Atmosphere

Let's learn about...

- composition of the atmosphere.
- structure of the atmosphere.
- solar insolation and terrestrial radiation.
- greenhouse effect.
- global warming and its impacts.
- measures for reducing global warming.

Key Terms

- atmosphere
- radiation
- global warming
- insolation
- ozone
- climate change

Reflect

When you see leaves rustling outside, what are you actually seeing? ....

Close your mouth and take a deep breath through your nose. What are you smelling? ....

Go outside, close your eyes and listen. What do you hear? ....

We know that the Earth is the only planet that supports life. The presence of life-supporting gases such as oxygen, nitrogen and carbon dioxide makes it a unique planet. All these gases are present in a gaseous layer that envelopes the Earth. This layer is known as the atmosphere.

The Earth's atmosphere is believed to have been formed by complex evolutionary processes. Water was present on the Earth billions of years ago. The air at that time contained large quantities of gases such as carbon dioxide and ammonia. There was no freely occurring oxygen in the air. The first organisms on the Earth survived without any oxygen. Gradually, these organisms started performing photosynthesis. This led to the accumulation of oxygen in the air and eventually the formation of the ozone layer. The atmosphere is not as dense as land or water but it has weight and exerts pressure. It is held to the Earth by its gravitational pull.

Composition of the Atmosphere

The atmosphere is composed of several different gases in varying amounts. Nitrogen, oxygen and argon are the permanent gases of the atmosphere and their percentages do not change from day to day.

evolutionary: relating to the gradual development of something

Nitrogen accounts for 78 per cent of the atmosphere, oxygen 21 per cent and argon 0.9 per cent. Gases like carbon dioxide, nitrous oxides, methane and ozone are trace gases that account for about a tenth of one per cent of the atmosphere. The concentration of water vapour in the atmosphere varies from 0 to 4 per cent of the atmosphere, depending on where we are and what time of the day it is. In the cold, dry Artic regions, water vapour usually accounts for less than 1 per cent of the atmosphere, while in the humid, tropical regions, water vapour can account for almost 4 per cent of the atmosphere. Water vapour content is very important in predicting weather.

Figure Out

Discuss the importance of green plants and their role in conserving the air around us. Go through science journals and find out about the nitrogen cycle and the oxygen cycle.

Each gas is essential to sustain life on Earth. Oxygen helps in respiration and burning. Nitrogen dilutes the concentration of oxygen and slows down the process of oxidation. Carbon dioxide is utilized by plants for photosynthesis to prepare food. These gases are present in a thin layer that protects the Earth from the intense heat of the Sun or the freezing cold from space.

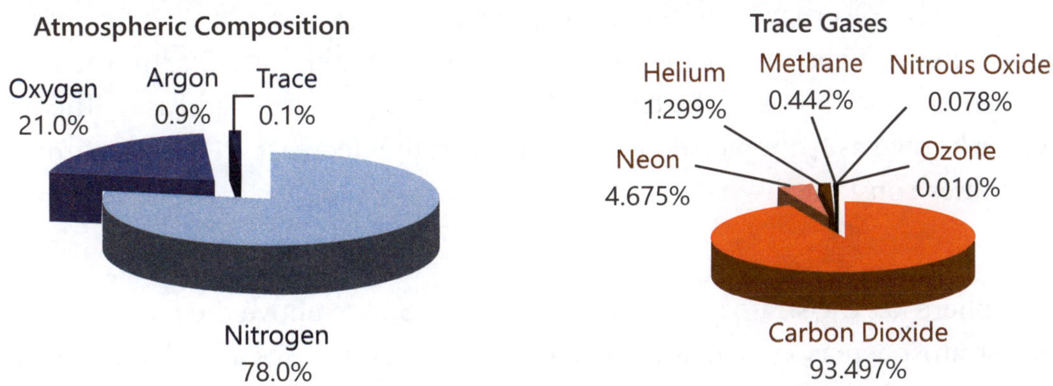

Composition of the atmosphere

The percentage of greenhouse gases present in the air varies daily, seasonally and annually. They have physical and chemical properties which make them interact with solar radiation and infrared light given off from the Earth to affect the energy balance of the globe. Although they are present in miniscule amounts in the Earth's atmosphere, they can strongly affect the global energy balance and temperature over time.

Green Earth

The Earth receives energy from the Sun mostly in the form of visible radiation. Some of this solar energy is reflected back to space as visible light and the rest is processed in various ways by the Earth, atmosphere and the oceans and re-radiated back to space in the form of infrared radiation (IR). This energy transformation determines the climatic conditions of the Earth.

Structure of the Atmosphere

The atmosphere consists of six layers—troposphere, stratosphere, mesosphere, thermosphere, exosphere and ionosphere. If you look at the diagram, you will see that the Earth's atmosphere is more like a five-layered cake. Each layer has its own composition, temperature and other characteristics.

trace gases: gases in the atmosphere other than nitrogen, oxygen and argon; global energy balance: the balance between incoming energy from the Sun and outgoing heat from the Earth

Troposphere

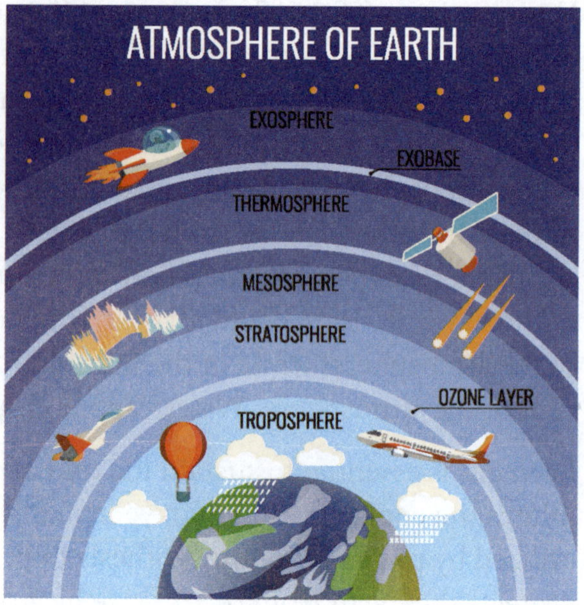

Layers of the atmosphere

The troposphere is the lowest layer of the atmosphere. This is the layer in which we live and where precipitation occurs. Its average height is between 10 to 11 km (15 to 16 km at the Equator, 5 to 6 km at the poles). It accounts for 75 to 80 per cent of the total mass of the Earth's atmosphere. All the day-to-day weather changes that we experience take place in the troposphere. Most of the water vapour and dust particles are found in this layer. This layer also acts as a blanket and prevents the days from becoming very hot and the nights from becoming very cold. Apart from water vapour, this layer also contains more carbon dioxide than the other layers. As carbon dioxide is the heaviest of all the gases in the air, it is found mostly in the lower layers of the troposphere. This helps support life as it absorbs the warmth from the Sun making the Earth warm. As we move upwards towards the higher levels of the troposphere, the temperature decreases. The upper limit of the troposphere is known as tropopause. As we go higher, the decrease in temperature stops and the temperature becomes constant.

Stratosphere

Above the troposphere lies the stratosphere. It extends from 50 km above the Earth's surface. The lower boundary of the stratosphere is known as the tropopause. When you see a jet flying high above in the sky, you will notice that the jet leaves behind a white trail as it moves on. Jet planes fly in this zone and the white trail is the moisture from the engine which condenses but is not disturbed as there is no air movement in this zone. Commercial jet planes fly in the lower stratosphere to avoid turbulence.

A portion of the stratosphere is called the ozonosphere as it contains the maximum concentration of ozone. Ozone protects us by absorbing the harmful ultraviolet rays of the Sun. Today, scientists are concerned about the depletion of this layer. The upper boundary of the stratosphere is called the stratopause.

Mesosphere

The mesosphere lies above the stratosphere. It extends to a height of about 80 km above the Earth's surface. Most of the meteors burn as they enter this sphere. In this layer, the temperature decreases as one moves up. The coldest temperatures in the Earth's atmosphere is about -90 degrees and is found in the top part of this layer.

Thermosphere

The fourth layer of the atmosphere is the thermosphere. The temperature rises rapidly in this layer as the high-energy X-ray and UV rays are absorbed in this layer. Most of the man-made satellites orbit the Earth within the thermosphere. The thermosphere extends to a height of about 450 km above the Earth's surface. The northern lights or aurora borealis occur in this sphere.

Exosphere

The outer-most layer of the atmosphere is the exosphere and it is said to be the 'final frontier' of the atmosphere. There is no definite boundary and the exosphere gradually fades to outer space.

Ionosphere

The ionosphere is not a distinct layer like the other layers of the atmosphere. It starts from 50 km and extends to about 1000 kms. Thus, this layer extends into both mesosphere and thermosphere. This is a region of high energy radiation from the Sun. The Sun breaks the molecules loose into electrically charged particles called ions. The ionosphere plays a very important role in communication. Radio waves used in long distance communications are reflected back to Earth in the ionosphere.

Solar Insolation

We know that the Sun is the chief source of heat and light. The Earth receives only a fraction of it from the Sun. The solar energy received by the Earth is known as insolation. When the Sun's rays reach the Earth, some of the heat warms up the surface while some bounces back in to space. This warms the atmosphere and is known as terrestrial radiation. As the atmosphere is heated mainly by terrestrial radiation, the air near to the Earth's surface has high temperature which decreases with an increase in altitude within the troposphere.

There is a cyclic movement of air near the Earth's surface. Let's see how it happens.

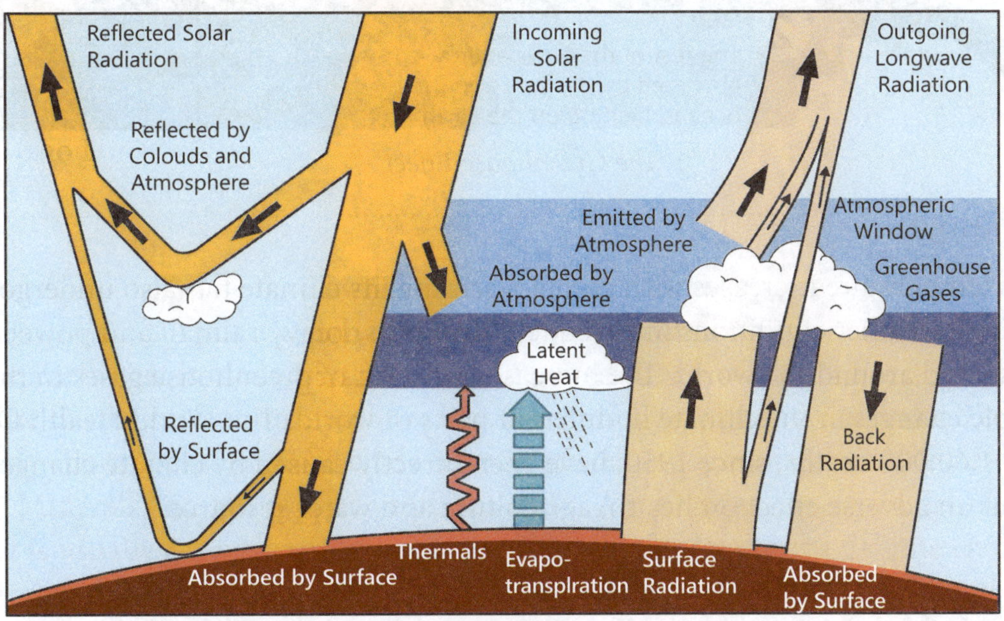

Solar insolation

The Greenhouse Effect

The greenhouse effect is a natural process that warms the Earth's surface. When the Sun's energy reaches the Earth's atmosphere, some of it is reflected back to space. The rest is absorbed by carbon dioxide and other greenhouse gases present in the atmosphere. These gases trap the heat and do not allow it to escape back into space. This is known as the greenhouse effect. This heating is required as it is essential for our survival. Carbon dioxide, methane and nitrous oxide are some greenhouse gases. However, gases that are emitted from a variety of industrial processes are increasing carbon dioxide and other heat trapping gases in the atmosphere, leading to a gradual rise in global temperature. This phenomenon is referred to as global warming. Our planet is gradually becoming warmer and has been a major concern for environmentalists worldwide. This is because it is believed that if the Earth becomes too warm, all the iceberg in the polar regions will melt. This would ultimately lead to an increase in the sea level and submerging of the coastal land. It is also believed that desert land will increase making life difficult for all living beings.

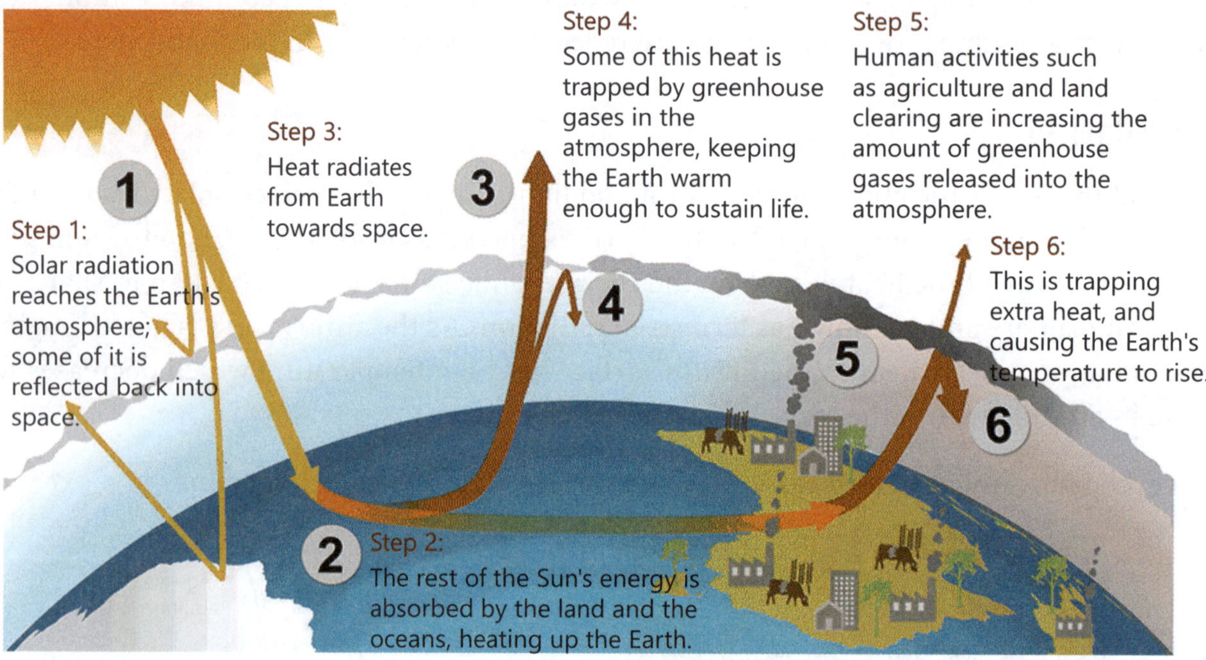

The Greenhouse Effect

Climate Change

As the Earth's temperature increases with global warming, its climate has also undergone drastic changes. Extreme weather conditions like frequent droughts, heavy rainfall and powerful hurricanes have been observed around the world. The increased portion of greenhouse gases in the atmosphere leads to variable changes in the climate in different parts of world. The World Health Organization estimates that 1,60,000 deaths, since 1950, have been directly caused by climate change. Climate change also has an adverse effect on health, agriculture and water resource.

Factors influencing climate change

The important factors that are responsible for climate change are greenhouse gases, deforestation, land use change, energy usage and vehicular usage.

Greenhouse gases

Human activities and industrialization have led to an increase in greenhouse gas (GHGs) emissions. The GHGs are considered the main cause of climate change on the Earth. The emission of GHGs beyond certain limits make the Earth's atmosphere hotter. Carbon dioxide is the most important

DIY

Study the table and answer the questions.

A comparison of greenhouse gas emissions by sector between 1994 and 2007 in million tons of carbon dioxide			
	1994	2007	Annual Growth Rate in %
Electricity	355.03 (28.4%)	719.30 (37.8%)	5.6
Transport	80.28 (6.4%)	142.04 (7.5%)	4.5
Residential	78.89 (6.3%)	137.84 (7.2%)	4.4
Other Energy	78.93 (6.3%)	100.87 (5.3%)	1.9
Cement	60.87 (4.9%)	129.92 (6.8%)	6.0
Iron & Steel	90.53 (7.2%)	117.32 (6.2%)	2.0
Other Industry	125.41 (10.0%)	165.31 (8.7%)	2.2
Agriculture	344.48 (27.5%)	334.41 (17.6%)	- 0.2
Waste	23.23 (1.9%)	57.73 (3.0%)	7.3

Source: INCCA- India: Greenhouse Gas Emission 2007

1. Why do you think agriculture accounted for the maximum amount of greenhouse gas emissions in 1994?
2. Which industry registered the greatest annual growth rate in emissions from 1994 to 2007?
3. What trend do you notice in gas emissions from 1994 to 2007?

GHG. It constitutes about 70 per cent of total GHG emissions. It originates from the burning of fossil fuel, deforestation, decay of biomass and agriculture. India contributes about 1.2 tons of carbon dioxide per capita. This is very insignificant as compared to the United States (20.6 tons), the United Kingdom (8 tons) and Japan (8 tons). The energy sector is one of the major producers of carbon dioxide in India. This is because around 58 per cent of energy needs are met from coal in India.

Deforestation

There is a considerable reduction in the forest cover due to encroachment, land use change, and economic development activities such as construction of roads, canals and power stations. Forests are the major source of carbon absorption and the hotspots of biodiversity. They act as the backbone of any environment and ecosystem. It is estimated that 77 to 68 per cent of the forest areas in India are likely to experience a shift in forest type.

Land-use change

A huge portion of forestland is being diverted for non-forest use. A relative growth in land-use change is also visible in urban and rural areas due to urbanization and industrialization. Fragmentation of forests and habitats is another major reason for loss of biodiversity.

Energy usage

Energy generation has grown manifold due to increasing demand. Coal, gas and diesel, being the major sources of power in India, are leading to increased emissions of GHGs. In addition to this, the unorganized sector is also engaged in power generation through low capacity diesel generator sets and coal-fired generators.

Vehicular Usage

Data reveals that there has been consistent growth in vehicular registration. The emission load depends on the type of vehicle. In India, we have standard and non-standard vehicular emissions, which also vary from place to place depending on regulatory mechanisms in use by the civic and local authorities in different areas. Some metropolitan cities have standards similar to the European Emission standards.

Impacts of climate change

The main impacts of climate change are:

Melting of glaciers: Due to global warming, glaciers have been observed to be melting steadily. Greenland has experienced glacial earthquakes which occur when a large mass of ice breaks off a glacier. This only happens in Greenland and Antarctica. Due to global warming, the frozen tundra in the Siberian region and the snow cover in the Arctic are melting rapidly. The Arctic snow cover is expected to be ice-free by 2037.

Warming of the ocean water: Oceanographers predict that the temperature of the ocean water will increase gradually due to which many marine species might die or will disappear leaving behind only the marine species that can survive in warmer climates.

Increase in the sea level: Due to global warming, the area of the sea-ice in both the poles will melt and shrink. It is expected that in the near future, this shrinking of the ice will lead to the increase in water level. The coastal areas might get submerged and suffer from tropical cyclones and hurricanes.

Shifting in farming regions: Geoscientists predict that regions in the low latitudes will have low agricultural yield in the near future. This may lead to food shortages in those regions. The agricultural yield will increase in the regions located in the middle and higher latitude. Thus, there is probability of a shift in farming regions from low latitudes to high latitudes.

Climatic changes: It is expected that land temperature will increase, maximum around the northern latitudes and minimum over the Southern Ocean. The frequency of hot waves will increase. These climatic changes will result in an increasing number of floods and droughts.

Measures to Reduce Global Warming

All over the world, people are coming together to find out ways to combat global warming. Global warming is a global issue thus, international organizations work together towards reducing the emissions worldwide. Scientists have found some technological and practical solutions to solve the problem. A comprehensive set of climatic solutions has been given by environmentalists to reduce carbon emissions.

Extensive use of renewable energy such as solar power, geothermal energy and hydel energy will reduce the use of fossil fuels which is considered to be a major source of carbon dioxide. Vehicles like lorries, trucks and vehicles carrying heavy loads emit carbon dioxide and other gases causing global warming. By increasing the vehicle fuel efficiency, emissions can be controlled thereby controlling its effects. The government has implemented policies to check and limit industries from emitting carbon dioxide. Plantation of trees, that is, afforestation and furthering the increase of forest habitats will improve the environment.

The atmosphere is one of the most important realms of the Earth. If we do not control pollution, it would be difficult for life to be sustained. Satellite images show a pattern of air pollutants entering the stratosphere and damaging the ozone layer. Let us all work together and make the Earth clean and green.

Geo Connect

Scientists believe that climate change, due to global warming, is going to affect Africa even if it does not face the threat of rapid industrialization. Africa is vulnerable to the impacts of global changes as it already experiences a hot and dry tropical climate. The economy of the continent is mostly dependent on the agricultural sector. Therefore, severe droughts will affect the economy of the continent. Climate change can also reduce its agricultural productivity.

In a Nutshell

- Atmosphere is the blanket of air that surrounds the Earth. It is divided into six main layers—troposphere, stratosphere, mesosphere, thermosphere, exosphere and ionosphere.
- All the weather phenomena take place in the troposphere.
- The atmosphere has gases that trap the Sun's heat by absorbing terrestrial radiation.
- The increase of the greenhouse gases in the atmosphere is leading to global warming.
- All over the world, people are coming together to find out ways to combat global warming.
- If we do not control pollution, it would be difficult for life to be sustained.

Workout

A. Fill in the blanks.

1. The atmosphere is held to the Earth by its ....
2. .... protects us by absorbing the harmful ultraviolet rays of the Sun.
3. High-energy X-ray and UV rays are absorbed in the ....
4. .... is the lowest layer of the atmosphere.

B. Fill in the blanks with the correct answers.

1. .... is used by plants for photosynthesis.
   a. Oxygen b. Carbon dioxide c. Nitrogen d. Argon
2. A portion of the stratosphere is called the .... as it contains the maximum concentration of ozone.
   a. ionosphere b. exosphere c. ozonospher d. stratopause
3. The .... fades into outer space.
   a. exosphere b. thermosphere c. ionosphere d. mesosphere
4. Radio waves are reflected back to the Earth from the ....
   a. ionosphere b. exosphere c. thermosphere d. stratosphere

C. Give reasons for the following.

1. Nitrogen is necessary in the atmosphere.
2. Global warming is an international concern.
3. There is a cyclonic movement near the Earth's surface .
4. Jet planes leave a trail behind as it moves.
5. The composition of the atmosphere is not the same everywhere.
6. The atmosphere is necessary for human survival.

D. Answer these questions in brief.

1. State the importance of the troposphere.
2. What do you mean by ozone depletion?
3. Differentiate between:
   a. insolation and terrestrial radiation
   b. troposphere and stratosphere
4. Why is the ozone layer important?

E. Answer these questions in detail.

1. How can we minimize the effects of global warming?
2. What do you mean by greenhouse effect?
3. How can greenhouse effect be reduced?
4. Describe in detail the adverse effects of global warming.

Think Box

As industries emit huge amounts of carbon dioxide, it is neccessary to put a check on them. Carbon tax is calculated on the basis of carbon emissions from the industry. Why do think the government has implemented this policy of paying carbon tax?

Picture Study

Look at this picture and answer the questions.

1. In which layer do aeroplanes fly?
2. In which layer do hot air balloons fly?
3. Which layer causes meteors to burn up?
4. Name the layer which plays an important role in radio communication.

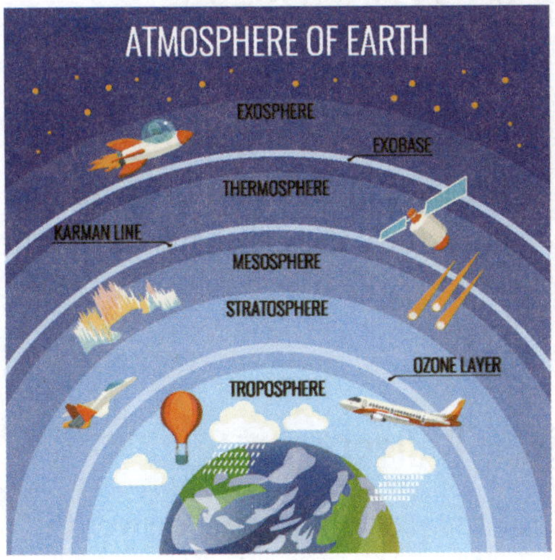

Life Skills and Values

The ozone layer is damaged by long term usage of chlorofluorocarbons, which are manufactured gases used in nearly all refrigerators and air conditioners. Organize a symposium/seminar to share and learn about the adverse effects of ozone depletion and how to combat it. Invite your science teacher and your social science teacher to evaluate your seminar.

Enjoy

The atmosphere is made up of different layers. Each layer has its own importance. Explore their importance. With the help of your geography and art teacher, make a clay model of the layers of the atmosphere. Put a flag in each layer and mention its respective importance.

Weblinks

For more information, visit
https://www.nasa.gov/mission_pages/sunearth/science/atmosphere-layers2.html
Last accessed on 31/July/2020

4 Weather and Climate

Let's learn about...

- weather and climate.
- elements of climate and weather.
- the uses of different instruments to record and study the elements of weather.

Key Terms

- weather
- climate
- temperature
- humidity
- precipitation
- atmospheric pressure

Reflect

Read the paragraph and answer the questions.

Manoj lives in a small coastal village in Kozhikode. He is a fisherman. The fishermen and women from his village were ready to go to sea for a fresh catch. One of them switched on the radio to check the weather forecast before heading to the sea. This is a regular practice in the village. The fishermen and women learnt from the radio report that they should be cautious while venturing into the sea as high tides in the range of 3 to 3.5 metres were expected at 23:30 hours along the Kerala coast between Vizhinjam and Kasargod.

- Why do you think the fishermen and women listen to the weather forecast before they venture out to the sea?
- Why do you think weather forecast is an important part of the news bulletin?
- Do you think the weather along the coast and the inland regions will vary?

We have read about weather and climate in the previous classes. Climate is one of the most basic elements of the natural environment. It has a great influence on our socio-cultural and economic activities. It affects the kind of clothes we wear, the food we eat, the types of houses we live in and the type of work we do.

FactPedia

The first meteorological observatories in India were established by the British East India Company. These included the Calcutta Observatory (1785), Madras Observatory (1796) and the Colaba Observatory (1826).

Weather is the day-to-day condition of the atmosphere at any place. It includes the temperature, rainfall, wind, humidity, sunshine, cloudiness and other such elements. Weather is dynamic in nature as it keeps changing. Thus, we can say that weather is the condition of the atmosphere at a particular place over a short period of time.

Climate is generally defined as the average state of weather over a long period of time. Various methodical observations, recordings and processing of elements such as humidity, winds, clouds, air pressure and sunshine is done before the standardization of the climate of a region. Moreover, climate is generally recorded for a larger region. For example, the equatorial climate is hot and humid with 4 o'clock showers. Thus, climate is defined as the average weather conditions of the temperature, atmospheric pressure, wind, humidity and precipitation of a large area over a long period of time.

Daily weather

The elements used for studying climate or the weather conditions of a place are the same.

The difference between weather and climate are as follows:

- Weather is the daily change of atmospheric condition whereas, climate is the atmospheric condition recorded over a long period of time.
- Weather always keeps changing whereas climate remains constant for a long period of time.
- Weather involves the study of temperature, humidity, rain, wind, pressure, cloud cover and sunshine whereas climate involves the study of daily weather recordings over a long period of time.
- The study of weather is known as meteorology whereas the study of climate is known as climatology.

Despite the differences, climate and weather do share one similarity, which is, that both their elements are temperature, pressure, wind, precipitation, sunshine and cloud cover.

Elements of Weather

The elements that determine the climate and the weather of a place are temperature, atmospheric pressure, humidity, clouds, precipitation and wind.

Temperature

Temperature is the term used to express the intensity or degree of heat. The Sun is the only natural source of heat energy for the Earth. The radiation from the Sun has three components—visible light, ultraviolet rays and infrared rays. There is an unequal distribution of solar energy on the Earth because of its spherical shape and inclined axis. Therefore, the amount of heat received at any place depends on the duration of the sunlight and the angle at which the Sun's rays fall on the Earth.

The temperature of a place is measured with the help of a thermometer. The Six's Thermometer, which was invented by James Six, automatically records the maximum and minimum temperature of a place during a period of twenty-four hours.

Generally, the temperature of a place is determined by the latitude, altitude, distance from the sea, wind, ocean currents, relief, slope of land, soil and vegetation cover.

Atmospheric pressure

The air has weight and it exerts pressure. The atmospheric pressure is the pressure that the atmosphere exerts on the surface of the Earth. When air expands, it creates a low-pressure area. Therefore, when the temperature is high, low pressure is created. When the temperature is low, air becomes heavier and denser creating high-pressure regions. Therefore, the difference in the atmospheric pressure causes the movement of the air. Severe weather phenomena such as thunderstorms, tornadoes and cyclones are all associated with the variations in the atmospheric pressure.

Wind

We have already learnt that wind is the horizontal movement of air. Winds blow from regions of high pressure to regions of low pressure. The greater the difference in pressure between two places, the faster the air will move.

FactPedia

Isobars are imaginary lines drawn on maps that join all the places that have equal atmospheric pressure.

The main cause of wind is the unequal heating of the atmosphere by the Sun resulting in differences in the pressure between places. How do you think scientists and meteorologists study wind? They do so by measuring the wind's direction and speed. An **anemometer** is used for measuring the speed of the wind. A **wind vane** is used to determine the direction of the wind. Winds are usually named after the direction they originate from. India is influenced by southeasterly monsoon winds. This implies that the monsoon winds originate from the southeastern direction. Thus, a wind coming from east to west is called an easterly wind.

If the Earth was stationary, the direction of all winds would have been north to south in the Northern Hemisphere. But the Earth moves from west to east and due to the rotation on its axis, the winds are deflected. This force is called **Coriolis force**. According to **Ferrell's Law**, winds are deflected towards the right in the Northern Hemisphere and towards the left in the Southern Hemisphere. Thus, a wind that would normally blow from north to south deflects towards the east. A good example of this are the northeast trade winds. The direction of the wind also affects the temperature of a place. Winds coming from warmer areas increase the temperature of a place whereas the winds coming from cooler regions decrease the temperature of a place. Regions near the deserts have high temperatures while the places near the poles have cold temperature.

Humidity

Humidity is the amount of moisture or water vapour present in the atmosphere. It is the amount of dampness in the atmosphere. We have already seen that the air around us always contains water vapour in varied amounts. For example, a damp cloth exposed to the air dries rapidly during the hot season as compared to the rainy season.

Humidity is of two types—**absolute humidity** and **relative humidity**. Absolute humidity is the total amount of water vapour present in a given volume of air. Relative humidity is the ratio of the amount of water vapour in a certain volume of air, and the maximum amount that might exist without condensation at a certain temperature. Relative humidity increases or decreases with the change in air temperature. For example, at a temperature of 0°C one cubic meter of air may contain 4.8 g of vapour. At a temperature of 30°C it will increase to 30.4 g. Thus, we can infer that the higher the temperature of the air, the more moisture it can absorb. The instrument used for measuring relative humidity is the **hygrometer** or wet and dry bulb thermometer. Relative humidity is expressed as a percentage. In each case, saturation point is taken as 100. If relative humidity is very high, the air is said to be moist. If the relative humidity is very low, the air is said to be dry.

Precipitation

We have already learnt that evaporation is a continuous process. The water bodies present on the surface of the Earth supply most of the moisture available in the atmosphere. We have also learnt that the capacity of the air to hold water depends largely on the temperature and increases with an increase in temperature. When warm air carrying water vapour rises up, it comes in to contact with the cooler layers of the atmosphere. The water vapour changes into small droplets of water. This process is known as **condensation**. When minute droplets of water or crystals join together to form drops or crystals which are too heavy to float, they start falling on the Earth as **precipitation**. Rain, snow, hail and sleet are some forms of precipitation.

> **Figure Out**
> Why do wooden doors shrink during winter and slightly increase in size during the rainy season?

The form of precipitation changes with the change of temperature. For example, rainfall is common in lower altitudes and snowfall in the higher altitudes. Rainfall is measured with a **rain gauge**. Rainfall is measured in millimeters or centimeters; the daily records are added for a year which is the total rainfall in one particular year. The average rainfall of a place for 35 to 40 years is called the **mean annual rainfall**.

Weather Instruments

Thermometer

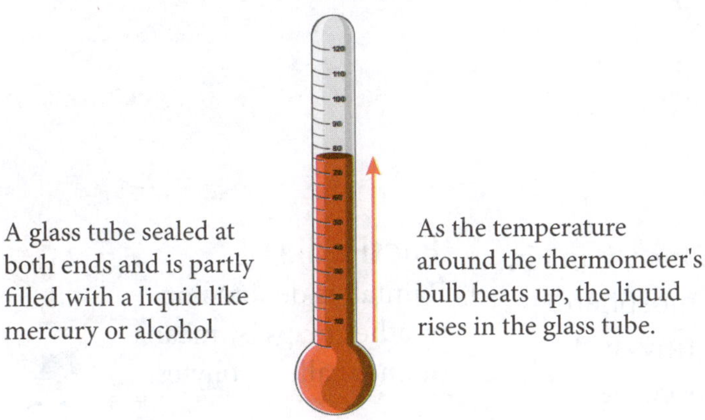

Barometer

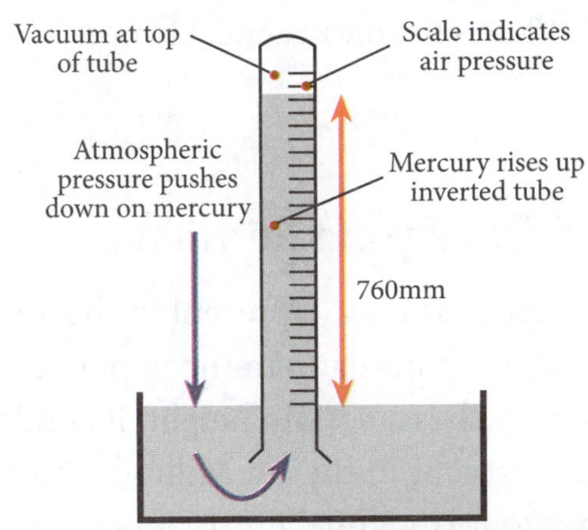

Rain gauge

Water that overflows into the outer cylinder is measured when rainfall exceeds an inch.

Hygrometer

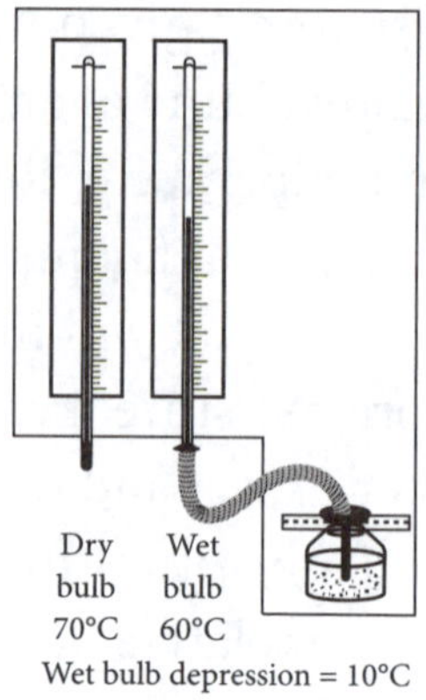

A hygrometer consists of two thermometers, one of which has its bulb constantly kept wet. Evaporation from the bulb lowers the temperature so this thermometer shows a lower temperature. Humidity is measured from the temperature shown by the dry bulb thermometer and the difference in temperature shown by the wet bulb and dry bulb thermometers.

Anemometer

The cups catch the wind and depending on how fast the axel is spinning, the wind speed is measured.

Wind Vane

When the wind is sufficiently strong, the head of the arrow will indicate the direction from which the wind is blowing.

DIY

Look at the table and answer the questions.

Station A is located at an altitude of 15 m above the sea level. The table shows the temperature and rainfall data.

Month	J	F	M	A	M	J	J	A	S	O	N	D
Temp in C	24.4	24.4	26.7	28.3	30.0	28.9	27.2	27.2	27.2	28.3	27.2	25.2
Rainfall in cm	0.25	—	—	—	—	50.2	59.2	40.0	27.2	5.1	1.0	—

1. What is the total annual rainfall?
2. Does the station lie near a sea coast? [Hint: study the range of temp. carefully]
3. What is the mean annual temperature?

Cloud Cover and Sunshine

Water vapour is always present in the air. As it is lighter than air, it rises and accumulates in the upper layer of the atmosphere. When it reaches a certain height, it condenses into tiny dust particles present in the air. Millions of such droplets come together to form white, fluffy clouds.

FactPedia

Rainfall is denoted on weather maps by means of lines called isohytes.

Clouds are masses of small water droplets or tiny ice crystals that float in the air. When clouds block the Sun, they appear grey. Weather conditions are influenced by cloud cover. For example, you must have experienced the difference between a cloudy day and a sunny day. Cloud cover reduces the amount of insolation and terrestrial radiations. Therefore, we are not exposed to direct sunlight. Clouds also trap heat near the surface of the Earth and do not allow the heat to escape back into the atmosphere. Therefore, we experience more hot and humid weather conditions during cloudy days than on cloudless days. Cloudless skies indicate fair weather conditions. On weather maps, an okta, which is a unit of measurement, is used to express the amount of cloud cover.

Types of clouds

Clouds are categorized as high, middle and low clouds depending on their height, appearance and vertical development.

The high clouds are of three types—cirrus, cirrocumulus and cirrostratus. The cirrus clouds are made of ice crystals. They are thin and wispy. They indicate fair weather. The cirroculmulus are small, rounded white puffs that exist individually or in longer rows. The cirrostratus are thin sheet-like clouds. We can see the Sun and the Moon clearly through them. They often appear right before any form of precipitation.

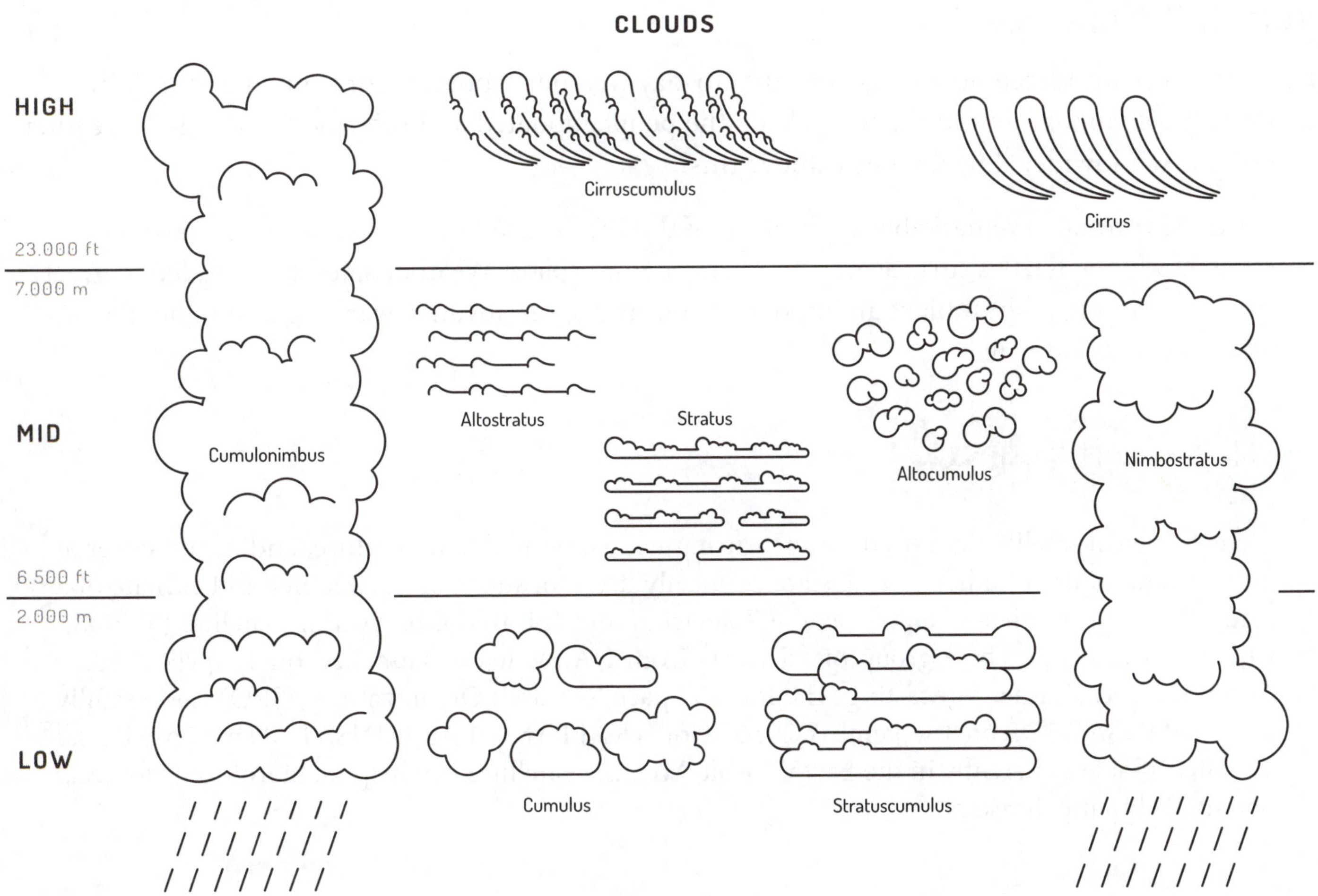

Types of clouds

The middle clouds are altostratus and altocumulus. The altostratus are mostly grey or bluish grey in color. They often cover the entire sky and appear puffy. They usually block the light coming from the Sun or the Moon resulting in the absence of shadows. The altoculmulus are mostly water droplets.

The low clouds include stratus, stratocumulus and nimbostratus. The stratus are uniform grey clouds. They resemble fog that does not reach the ground. They usually cause no precipitation with the exception of a light drizzle or mist. The stratocumulus are low lumpy clouds. The nimbostratus are dark grey clouds. They cause continuous rain or snowfall.

The duration of sunshine also plays an important role in determining the weather or climate of a place. Places near the tropics experience more abundant sunshine compared to the places in the temperate latitude regions. In India, during the summer season, more hours of sunshine is experienced than the winter season. There are several instruments that measure the duration of sunshine. In the Campbell-Stokes Sunshine Recorder, the Sun's rays are concentrated on a chemically sensitized card with spherical lens. This card generates a pattern as the Sun moves across the sky during the hours of bright sunshine.

Campbell-Stokes Sunshine Recorder

Role of Technology

Have you ever wondered how we get our day-to-day weather reports incorporated in our daily news? News channels around the world keep the people updated and informed of the daily weather conditions worldwide. How do they achieve this?

This is done through a remarkable application of the Earth's satellites. These satellites have the ability to study the Earth's surface and cloud cover from space. Weather satellites have led to great advances in meteorology. It plays an important role as it gives advance warning of potentially dangerous tropical storms.

Geo Connect

Meteorological satellites are used for measuring winds, rainfall, temperature, and cloud cover at frequent intervals. Weather satellites are primarily used for monitoring weather and climate of a place. The first weather satellite was the Television and Infrared Observation Satellite (TIROS), which was developed by a group of scientists from NASA. It was launched on 1 April, 1960. It revolutionized weather forecasting. The Indian Space Research Organization (ISRO), successfully launched INSAT-3DR on 8 September, 2016. It joins KALPANA-1 AND INSAT-3D meteorological satellites, that are currently in the Earth's orbit. Weather satellites can help meteorologists forecast potential climatic disasters.

spherical: shaped like a sphere

In a Nutshell

- Weather and climate are closely related to each other.
- Weather refers to the atmospheric conditions of a small area for a short period of time, usually one day.
- Climate is the average state of weather over a long period of time.
- The elements of weather and climate are temperature, atmospheric pressure, humidity, precipitation and the direction of the wind.
- The factors that control the temperature of a place are latitude, altitude, distance from the sea, soil, vegetation and slope of the land.
- Thermometer, barometer, rain gauge, hygrometer, anemometer and wind vane are some weather instruments that we use.
- Clouds are categorized as high, middle and low clouds depending on their height, appearance and vertical development.
- Weather satellites have led to great advances in meteorology.

Workout

A. Fill in the blanks with the correct answers.

1. A thermometer is used to measure ....
   a. temperature b. pressure c. cloud cover
2. Temperature does not depend on ....
   a. latitude b. ocean current c. population density
3. Cloud cover is measured in ....
   a. degrees b. oktas c. percentage
4. Increase in temperature leads to a .... in humidity.
   a. increase b. decrease c. no change
5. Atmospheric pressure is measured by a ....
   a. thermometer b. barometer c. wind vane

B. Fill in the blanks.

1. When relative humidity is high, the air is said to be ....
2. .... is a type of high cloud.
3. The winds get deflected towards the right in the ....
4. Sunshine is measured by using ....
5. .... force is generated due to the rotation of the earth.

C. Answer these questions in brief.

1. State the factors that determine the temperature of a place.
2. What is the Coriolis Force?

3. What is the Ferrell's Law?
4. What are the different types of precipitation?
6. How is cloud cover shown on weather maps?

D. Answer these questions in detail.

1. Define humidity. How is it related to temperature?
2. Explain how cloud cover affects the weather of a place.
3. Explain precipitation as an important element of weather.
4. Explain the difference between weather and climate.

Think Box

Why does the air in the equatorial regions have more moisture than the desert regions?

Picture Study

Look at this picture and answer the questions.

1. Name the instrument.
2. Which element of weather does it measure?
3. Name another instrument which is used for a similar purpose.

Life Skills and Values

Create a journal about the precautions one should take in the following situations.

1. Humidity is low
2. Temperature is high
3. Heavy snowfall

Enjoy

Observe the clouds in the sky for a week. Draw the shape of the cloud in your notebook along with the date and time. After a week, write the type of cloud that you noticed on each day.

Weblinks

For more information, visit
https://oceanservice.noaa.gov/facts/weather_climate.html
Last accessed on 31/July/2020

5 Weathering and Soil Formation

Let's learn about...

- types of rocks.
- agents of gradation.
- weathering and its types.
- soil formation and soil profile.
- soil erosion and soil conservation.

Key Terms

- weathering
- agents of gradation
- minerals
- soil
- rocks
- soil profile

Reflect

I am the hardest part of the Earth and I form the major part of the Earth's surface. I break to form fertile land. All the important heritage monuments like the Taj Mahal are made of me. People derive important minerals from me and call me 'ore'. You can find me lying along the road side or by the side of the river as 'pebble' or 'boulder'. You ignore me most of the time but I am precious too.

Can you guess who I am?

....

The layer of the Earth that is made up of rocks is known as the lithosphere. The lithosphere is the solid crust of the Earth's surface on which we live. To carefully study and understand earth sciences, we need to study about rocks. Rocks include the soft as well as loose materials like clay, sand, gravel and silt. Minerals and soil are derived from rocks. A rock does not have a definite chemical composition. It is usually a mixture of various materials. Rocks that have a definite chemical composition and are mined for extraction of metals are called ores. For example, aluminum is extracted from bauxite.

Types of Rocks

Rocks occurs mainly in three types based on their formation. They are igneous rocks, sedimentary rocks and metamorphic rocks. Let us learn about them.

1. Igneous rock

Granite is an igneous rock

2. Sedimentary rock

Flint is a sedimentary rock

3. Metamorphic rock

Quartzite is a sedimentary rock

All these rocks differ from each other. They have their specific mode of origin, occurrence and chemical and physical properties.

Rock formation

Types of rocks	Formation	Name derived from.	Types based on origin of the rocks	Associated minerals/ores
Igneous Rocks	They are formed when the molten magma from the Earth's interior cools and solidifies.	Derived its name from the Latin word *ignis* meaning 'fire'; they are also known as primary rocks	**Intrusive Igneous rocks:** Solidified within the Earth's surface **Extrusive Igneous rocks:** Magma solidified on the Earth's surface	Granite, diorite, gabbro, basalt, pegmatite, volcanic breccia

Sedimentary Rocks	They are formed by transportation, deposition, sedimentation and cementation of sediments. This process is called **lithification.**	Derived its name from the Latin word *sedimentum* which means 'settling'	Sedimentary rocks are classified as: ■ Mechanically formed ■ Organically formed ■ Chemically formed	Conglomerate, sandstone, siltstone, shale, rock salt, iron ore, chert, flint, dolomite, limestone and coal
Metamorphic Rocks	These rocks are formed under the action of high pressure and temperature.	The word metamorphic means 'change of form'. It is derived from two words morph and meta.	Metamorphic rocks are of two major groups: **Foliated rocks:** They have a layered or banded appearance. **Non-Foliated rocks:** They do not have layers or bands.	Quartzite, slate, gneiss, schist, marble, gneissoid; valuable minerals like gold and silver are associated with metamorphic rocks.

Gradation

Gradation, derived from the Latin word *gradation*, is the process that levels land surfaces and includes simultaneous removal and deposition of Earth's particles.

You have seen earlier that the Northern Plains are formed by deposition brought down from the Himalayas and other such examples. Natural forces like running water, wind and tidal waves that bring about gradation are said to be agents of gradation. The process of gradation continuously works to level the Earth's surface. Denudation is a slow and continuous process. It works to wear away the covering rocks to expose the underlying rocks.

FactPedia

The Aravalli Range in Rajasthan is said to be an old fold mountain whose height is reducing with geological time. Geologists believe that agents of gradation, that have acted for millions of years, are responsible for reducing its height.

Gradation can be studied as:

- **Degradation:** The process by which the Earth's surface is lowered down by the agents of gradation
- **Aggradation:** The deposition of particles brought down by the agents of erosion; low lands are being filled up to level the surface due to this phenomenon.

Denudation, though a slow process, makes the Earth as we see it today.

Weathering

Weathering is the fracturing or disintegration and decomposition of rocks by natural agents. Weathering occurs in situ. That is, it is a static process and there is no movement except when the pieces of rocks fall under the force of gravity in their vicinity. The factors that influence the

in situ: in the appropriate position; vicinity: area around a particular place weathering of rocks are local climate, mineral composition of the rock, structure of the rock, vegetation, amount of exposed or bare rock surface and human activities. Weathering causes the modification of major landforms and formation of varied landscapes.

Types of Weathering

Weathering is mainly of three kinds—mechanical weathering, chemical weathering and biological weathering. Usually, it is difficult to differentiate between these three types of weathering as they are interrelated. Let us learn about them.

Mechanical weathering

Mechanical or physical weathering is the physical disintegration of rocks due to heat, water and frost. This type of weathering does not cause any change in the chemical composition of the rock. There are various agents that disintegrate the rocks.

Physical weathering

After a rain shower or snowfall, some of the water or snow collects in the cracks and cervices of rocks. In places of low temperatures, water turns to ice. When this happens, it expands. Once the ice expands during the night, it causes cracks in the rocks. This is known as frost shattering. This type of weathering creates sharp pinnacles on mountains peaks. Some angular fragments collect at the foot of mountain slopes to form scree or talus slope. In the daytime, ice melts into water and continues seeping further into the rocks. This alternative freezing and thawing soon widens the cracks and the rocks ultimately disintegrate.

In the desert regions, we find vast differences between the day and night temperatures. In the daytime, the temperature may rise and exceed 50 degrees centigrade and in the night, it may fall to freezing point. The minerals present in the rocks absorb heat at various rates and the rocks expand during the day. During the night, when the temperature dips to the minimum, the rocks contract.

Frost Shattering

Alternate contraction and expansion over a long period of time creates cracks and joints in the rocks. This is called block disintegration. The rocks then start to split along the cracks and joints. Slowly the entire rock splits into large blocks. When repeated expansion and contraction result in the disintegration of rocks into small pieces, it is called granular disintegration.

Exfoliation is the peeling of the outer layer of the rocks. The outer layer of rock is heated up and expands during the day while the inner rock layer remains cool. The outer layers eventually peel off, exposing the inner layers for further exfoliation.

Exfoliation

Chemical weathering

Chemical weathering involves changes in the chemical composition of rocks which lead to disintegration of the rocks into smaller pieces. Rainwater is an important agent in chemical weathering. Chemical weathering is more prominent in warm tropical regions. Carbon dioxide and water are the two most common chemical weathering agents. Carbon dioxide mixes with water to form carbonic acid that is able to dissolve the rock minerals. Rainwater contains dissolved carbon dioxide, forming a weak solution of carbonic acid. Rocks are made up of small particles and water has the ability to flow through these particles. The water containing carbon dioxide and other gases can dissolve or alter the chemical composition of the rocks. Limestone contains calcium carbonate which dissolves easily in water. Similarly, water can change feldspar to clay, sand and carbonates. Oxygen easily reacts with iron to form a flaky brown oxide. Rainwater reacts with the rocks that contain iron compounds.

Biological weathering

Plants, animals and human beings are agents of biological weathering. Growing plant roots penetrate into rocks, widen cracks and joints of rocks and split rocks apart. Plants such as mosses and lichens add moisture content to the rocks. This catalyzes the chemical reaction inside the rocks. Rodents and earthworms also cause the joints of rocks to loosen up. Uncovered rocks are subjected to agents of weathering like water and wind waves. Certain bacteria in the presence of water break down rock minerals and cause weathering. Human activities such as quarrying or mining cause large-scale disintegration of rocks.

Roots of the plants also cause weathering

Soil

We know that weathering involves the breaking and disintegration of rocks. What happens when the rocks are continuously broken down? The fragments of these disintegrated rock particles form soil.

feldspar: any of a group of hard rock-forming minerals

Soil is the thin surface layer of the Earth, comprising mineral particles formed by the breakdown of rocks and decayed organic matter. Soil formation starts with the weathering of rock masses and accumulation of weathered particles on the surface of the rock masses. These are called in situ soils. The components of soil are found in all three states of matter. The solid part is made of rock particles and humus. Humus, animals and insects living in the soil form organic matter. Air and soil water fills in the open spaces between the soil particles. Soil water contains dissolved salts, minerals and nutrients required by plants.

Figure Out

What type of rock formations are created due to erosion?

The rock which weathers to form soil is called bedrock. The soil gets its colour and mineral content from the minerals present in the bedrock. Several factors such as parent material, climate, living organisms, relief and time affect the weathering of the bedrock. Parent material is the rock which undergoes weathering. Climatic conditions like heat, rain and humidity determine the kind of weathering which will occur. Vegetation, bacteria and animals add to the organic content of the soil. Mountains, hills and plateaus have thin soil cover as the weathered particles collect near the slopes. Lowlands have a thicker soil cover.

Factors affecting the formation of soil

The factors that affect the formation of soil are the topography, the presence of organic matter, the time taken for the formation of soil and the composition of minerals. For example, alluvial soil is found in the Northern Plains whereas the Deccan Plateau has black soil. Let us learn more about the factors that influence the formation of soil.

- Plants, animals and other microorganisms determine the rate of humus formation and influence the fertility of the soil.
- The parent rock determines the physical properties such as colour, texture, chemical properties and mineral composition of the soil.
- Relief features such as the slope of the land and altitude determine the accumulation of soil.
- Time determines the thickness of the soil profile.

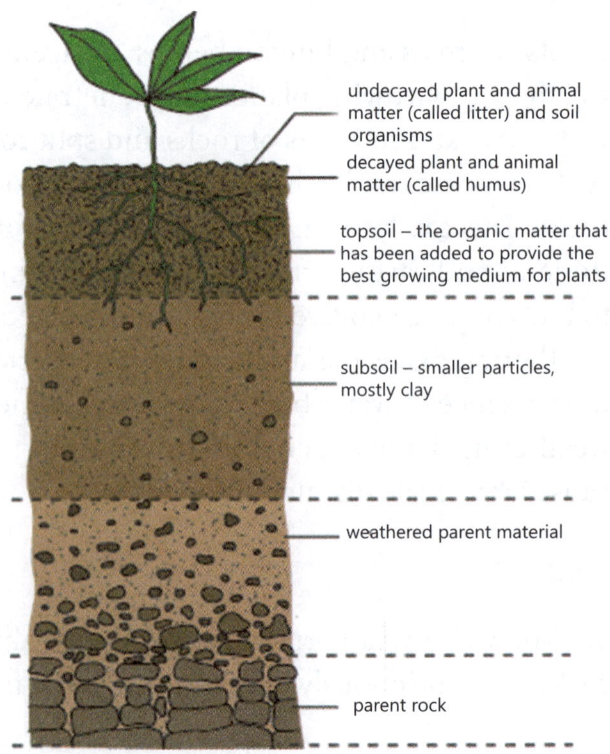

Soil Profile

Soil Profile

A vertical section of the soil showing its different layers is called a soil profile. Each layer has a different colour. Generally, a soil profile has four horizons. The uppermost layer containing organic matter and humus is called top soil. It is made of fine particles of clay, silt, sand, humus, salts, minerals and nutrients. The layer below the top soil is called the sub soil. It contains weathered rock material, sand, silt and clay.

This layer contains salts, minerals and traces of humus. The third layer is called the substratum and consists of large fragments of weathered parent rock material. The last layer is the bedrock which is not weathered. It provides a base to the other three layers.

Based on its formation, soil can be of two types—residual soil and transported soil. Residual soil is formed from the weathered rock. For example, black soil of the Deccan Plateau is formed from weathering of the volcanic basalt. Mechanical weathering of rocks forms the sandy soil of the desert region. Red soil is formed in situ by the decomposition of metamorphic rocks. Transported soil is formed when eroded rock materials are deposited in another place by the various agents of gradation. For example, alluvial soil is formed by the silt brought by rivers.

Importance of Soil

Soil is a vital natural resource. The fertility of the soil is determined by its capacity to support plant life. Artificial fertilizers are sometimes used to make the soil fertile. However, the excessive use of fertilizers leads to soil degradation. The overutilization of soil leads to its depletion disturbing the natural balance between soil formation and soil utilization.

Some of the factors that make soil fertile are:

- Minerals such as potash, nitrogen, silica and iron that are necessary for the growth of plants.
- Humus is the organic matter which is formed from dead and decaying vegetative matter.
- Plants absorb nutrients dissolved in water. Thus, soil should have adequate moisture content.
- Soil should be well aerated facilitating oxygen circulation.

DIY

Soil means something different for each of us. What do you think soil means to these people?

a. Farmer: ....

b. Construction worker: ....

c. Civil engineer: ....

d. Geologist: ....

e. Earthworm: ....

f. Owner of a dry cleaning business: ....

g. Bird: ....

h. Hydrologist: ....

i. Maple tree: ....

j. You: ....

Soil that loses its plant cover and is exposed to agents of gradation may be washed out or blown away. The removal of the fertile top soil by agents of erosion like rainwater, rivers, wind and waves is called soil erosion. Wrong agricultural practices like exercising the use of chemical fertilizers and pesticides deplete the quality of the soil.

Types of Soil Erosion

The three most common agents of soil erosion are running water, wind and human action.

Running water

The absence of vegetation and the slope of the land increases the rate of erosion. The roots of the plants hold the soil in place and allow the rainwater to percolate into the soil. When forests are cut down and the vegetation is removed, the rainwater cannot percolate into the soil and carry the top soil away. This is called sheet erosion. After several layers of topsoil are removed, small depressions form on the surface, creating an uneven surface. These depressions are called gullies. Gullies are widened by the action of flowing water. This creates large areas called badlands or ravines. The Chambal Valley in Madhya Pradesh is an example.

Wind action

Wind carries away loose topsoil in regions with no vegetation cover. Wind erosion causes massive destruction in the regions with scanty rainfall. It is common in desert regions.

> **Green Earth**
>
> Afforestation means planting trees in large numbers, especially in regions where forests have been cleared for agricultural purposes. *Van Mahotsav* is an annual tree plantation movement in India. Thousands of plants and trees are planted in different parts of India.

Human action

Defective farming techniques and removal of the natural vegetation increase the action of natural agents of erosion such as wind and water. Overgrazing is also one of the main causes of soil erosion.

Soil Conservation

Terrace farming

Soil conservation means to protect the topsoil from being eroded. The following measures can be taken to avoid soil erosion:

Contour ploughing: Sloping land is always ploughed across the slope to allow water to sink into the furrows. Ploughing parallel to the contour lines can control the flow of running water down the slopes.

Terrace farming: In the hilly regions, crops are grown in steps or terraces cut along the slope of the hills so that flat land is available for cultivation. At the edge of each terrace, a low mud wall called a bund is built to stop the flow of the rain down the slope.

Contour barriers: Bunds made using stones, grass, and soil can be used to build barriers along contour. Bunds should be constructed according to contours to restrict the flow of water.

percolate: to move gradually through a surface that has very small holes or spaces in it; furrows: long narrow cuts in the ground made to plant seeds

Plugging of gullies: Small dams of stone and soil are built across gullies to hold back the rainwater. This measure checks gullies from being widened and deepened further.

Shelter belts: Shelter belts are built in the desert regions to reduce soil erosion caused by wind action. Rows of trees are planted in order to reduce the speed of the winds so that the soil particles cannot be picked up and carried away. Such shelter belts are found in Rajasthan and sometimes even in the coastal regions.

Mulching: Mulching means covering. The bare ground is covered with a layer of organic matter like straw and husk to retain soil moisture.

Prevention of overgrazing: Grazing animals should be moved over different pastures so as to prevent the loss of vegetation cover on a particular patch of land. This would reduce soil erosion.

Soil conservation is of great concern to everyone all over the world. Efforts have been made by scientists and governments to protect the soil cover. In India, we mainly have alluvial soil, black soil, red soil, laterite soil and desert soil. Soil is usually classified based on its texture and colour which it mainly derives from the parent rock material. It is the medium which supports plants which in turn provides food for all living beings directly or indirectly. Thus, all living creatures depend directly or indirectly on the soil.

Geo Connect

Soil erosion and water degradation is one of the major environmental issues of the Latin American and Caribbean regions. These regions have the world's greatest reserve of arable land. The massive forest cover in these regions is declining rapidly because of overwhelming agricultural activity. This has enhanced the agricultural productivity but has also led to soil erosion, water degradation and depletion of biodiversity, leading to deforestation and environmental degradation. The countries of these regions are practising conservation agriculture. Conservation agriculture is a type of agricultural practice that involves minimum soil disturbance.

In a Nutshell

- Weathering is a process of breaking down or disintegration of exposed rocks by natural as well as human activity.
- There are three types of weathering—mechanical weathering, chemical weathering and biological weathering.
- A vertical section of the soil showing its different layers is called a soil profile. Each layer has a different colour.
- Soil formation occurs because of weathering.
- The three most common agents of soil erosion are running water, wind and human action.
- Soil is an important resource and conservation of soil is essential.

Workout

A. Fill in the blanks.

1. The vertical section of the soil is called ....
2. The process involved in transporting the weathered materials elsewhere by agents like water and wind is called ....
3. Mulching means ....
4. Aluminum is extracted from ....

B. Write one word for the following.

1. A process by which rocks break down because of the actions of rain, frost and changes in temperature: ....
2. The protection of the topsoil cover from removal: ....
3. Peeling of outer layer of rock: ....
4. Primary rocks: ....

C. Choose the correct answers and fill in the blanks.

1. .... is the washing away of layers of soil by various agents of erosion.
   a. Soil erosion b. Soil conservation c. Soil destruction d. Soil draining
2. Terrace farming is done on ....
   a. gentle slopes b. plain land c. steep slope d. deserts
3. Soil formed due to weathering in situ is ....
   a. red soil b. laterite soil c. black soil d. mud
4. There are .... types of weathering.
   a. three b. ten c. five d. two

D. Give reasons for the following.

1. Human activities are responsible for soil erosion.
2. Soil conservation is important.
3. In desert regions, rocks contract at night.
4. Wind action leads to soil erosion.

E. Answer these questions in brief.

1. What are igneous rocks?
2. Define granular disintegration.
3. What is gully erosion?
4. How does frost cause weathering?
5. Differentiate between sheet erosion and gully erosion.

F. Answer these questions in detail.

1. Explain the difference between rocks and minerals.
2. Explain any three factors that affect weathering.

3. Explain the formation of igneous rocks.
4. Explain the different types of soil conservation methods.
5. Explain the importance of soil.

Think Box

How are earthworms beneficial for the soil?

Picture Study

Look at this picture and answer the questions.

1. What do you see in the picture?
2. How does this activity affect the quality of soil?

Life Skills and Values

What do you know about the Chipko movement? Discuss how community can play an important role in the conservation of the environment.

Enjoy

Imagine that you are a pedologist, that is, a person who studies soil. You have to find the rate of erosion on cultivated and uncultivated portions of land. However, since you cannot visit the actual sites, you can do this experiment at home.

Steps:

1. Take two identical earthen trays and fill them up with similar quantities of soil.
2. Plant a few seeds of gram in one of the trays.
3. Keep the tray aside for a few days until the saplings have grown a few centimetres.
4. Place the two trays in front of a table fan and observe in which tray the soil is loose and blows away easily.

Note down your observations and write a conclusion. Present your report in the classroom.

Weblinks

For more information, visit
http://www.bbc.co.uk/bitesize/ks3/science/environment_earth_universe/rock_cycle/activity/
Last accessed on 31/July/2020

Theme 3

Human and Economic Geography

We know that physical geography deals with landforms, soil, atmosphere and other such gifts of nature, which influence human life on Earth. On the other hand, human and economic geography deals with certain economic activities such as manufacturing and trading of goods. It also gives us knowledge about the distribution of natural resources and their utilization for the development of human life on Earth. In the coming chapters, you will learn about the utilization of natural resources by studying about different economic activities like manufacturing industries and the harnessing of energy resources.

6 Industries

Let's learn about...

- classification of industries.
- factors influencing the location of industries.
- Special Economic Zones.
- industrial regions of India and the world.
- industrial pollution and environmental degradation.

Key Terms

- small scale industries
- large scale industries
- public sector
- private sector
- joint sector
- SEZ
- agro based
- marine based

Reflect

Where do you think the following products that you use are created?

1. Shirt ....
2. Newspaper ....
3. Bread ....

Manufacturing is the production of goods in large quantities after processing raw materials to more valuable and usable products. For example, paper is manufactured by processing raw materials such as wood. Similarly, sugar is manufactured by processing sugarcane. As opposed to wood and sugarcane, paper and sugar are more valuable because they can be used directly in many industries.

The manufacturing sector can be considered to be the backbone of the economic development of a country. In India, where agriculture is the occupation of a considerable population, the manufacturing sector provides a large number of jobs to the people.

Classification of Industries

We find many different things in a market. Do they all come from the same industry and are they made in the same place? Each of these items come from different sources and have different manufacturing processes. This is why we need to classify them into different industries. Industries can be classified on the basis of certain characteristics such as raw material, size and ownership.

Based on raw materials

Based on the raw material being used, industries can be classified as agro-based, marine-based, forest-based and mineral-based.

- Agro-based industries get their raw materials from plants and animals. Food processing, vegetable oil, cotton textile, dairy products and leather industries are agro-based industries. An example of an agro-based industry in India is the silk industry of Assam. It is very famous all over the world. Four types of silk worms are cultured—tassar, mulberry, muga and eri. Muga silk is one of the most popular products in India.
- The industries that derive raw materials from the sea and ocean are called marine-based industries. The seafood industry is an example.
- The industries that use forest produce as raw materials are forest-based industries. Pulp and paper, pharmaceuticals, furniture and construction materials are some forest-based industries. The northeastern states of India are famous for their forest-based industries. Several kinds of bamboo is found in this region. The products made from bamboo are baskets, mats, hats and furniture. Essential oils extracted from the eucalyptus tree is also a forest-based product.
- Mineral-based industries use minerals as raw materials. Iron and steel, cement, aluminum, machine tools and petrochemicals are mineral based-industries. The northeastern states of India have a considerable number of tea and petroleum industries. Assam is a major producer of crude petroleum. The four major oil refineries of this region are located in Guwahati, Digboi, Numaligarh and Bongaigaon. Petrochemical industries are located in Namrup and Bongaigaon.

A seafood market

A pharmaceutical lab

A jute plantation worker

Based on size

Size refers to the amount of people employed and the amount of money invested in the industry. Based on size, industries can be classified as small and large-scale industries.

- Small-scale industries use less amount of money and technology compared to a large industry. Cottage industries or household industries are small-scale industries. Pottery and basket-weaving are some examples. The cottage industry is one of the main sources of income for rural India. For example, small-scale industries play an important role in the economic development of the northeastern region of India. Manipur has the largest weaving industry. This industry is dominated by women and it is believed that almost every family in Manipur runs a loom. Weaving is also an important industry of Arunachal Pradesh. Metal bell work is also an important traditional industry of the northeastern states. Brass work is the most popular amongst them.

- Large-scale industries produce a large number of products and require huge investment. Technology is an important requirement for the large-scale industry. Automobile and heavy machinery are large scale industries. Large-scale industries are the economic backbone of our country. The government of India spends huge amounts of money in the development of large-scale industries as it in turn supports the growth of the small-scale industry. In India, large-scale industries are fertilizers, power, oil, gas and information technology. The Indian economy depends heavily on large-scale industries for growth. The Steel Authority of India Limited (SAIL), Oil and Natural Gas Corporation (ONGC), and Bharat Heavy Electricals Limited (BHEL) are some examples of large-scale industries in India.

Based on ownership

Ownership refers to the person or group of people who own the industry. Based on ownership, industries can be classified into private sector, public sector, joint sector and cooperative sector industries.

- The private sector industries are owned by individuals or groups of individuals. For example, Tata Steel Limited, Reliance Industries and Dabur are private sector industries.
- The public sector industries are owned and operated by government agencies. For example, the Steel Authority of India Limited (SAIL), Coal Authority of India Limited, and Hindustan Aeronautics Limited (HAL) are public sector industries.
- Joint sector industries are jointly run by the state and individuals or a group of individuals. Cochin Refiners Limited, Maruti Suzuki and Goa Carbon Limited are some examples.
- Cooperative sector industries are owned and operated by a group of people who are generally producers of raw materials or workers of that particular industry. For example, a sugar mill owned and run by farmers producing sugarcane. Cotton textile industry mostly functions as a cooperative sector industry.

Major Industries of the World

Major industries	Role of the industry in economic and industrial development	Location
Iron and Steel Industry	It is known as a basic industry because other industries such as automobile, shipbuilding, machine and tools depend on it for raw materials. Steel production is an index of national prosperity due to its extensive application as compared to other metals.	China, Japan, India, USA and Russia

Cotton Textile	Cotton is known as the 'king of all fibre'. It is one of the most widely distributed industries as there is a constant demand of textiles all over the world.	China, India, USA, Pakistan, Brazil, Japan
Information Technology	The information technology industry deals with all aspects of information based on computers. It includes both hardware and software technology which have become integral to every industry. These days, IT industries serve as an efficient medium of E-governance as it provides transparency and easy accessibility to information.	Finland, Singapore, Sweden, Norway, the Netherlands, Hong Kong, USA, South Korea, UK and India
Shipbuilding	It is essentially an industry on which a wide variety of parts are assembled to form a complete ship. Ships are large and expensive so they are usually built in small numbers. Ships are required for commercial purposes and for defense. It is also referred as naval engineering.	South Korea, Japan, USA, UK
Fishing	Fishing includes all kinds of human activities related to both aquatic animals in marine and inland waters all over the world. Fish is a vital source of food and the industry involves catching of fishes and processing of the fish. The fishing industry stimulates growth of the shipbuilding industry, manufacturing of nets and other equipment to catch and store the catch, and construction of boxes, tin cans and preservatives for packing.	China, India, Indonesia, Peru, Chile, Japan, Thailand and other European countries
Automobile	Like shipbuilding, the automobile industry involves a wide range of assembling of the component parts. This industry is involved in the production of both commercial vehicles like huge trucks to private vehicles like small cars. Its plays an important role in the development of the infrastructure of an economy.	Japan, USA, Germany, France

Factors Affecting the Location of Industries

The location of industries is determined by the availability of raw materials, power, labour, capital, transport and accessibility to the market. Most industries are located in regions where one or more of these factors are present.

Availability of raw materials: Industries which are based on bulky or perishable raw materials like mineral-based industries are located near the source of the raw material. An example is the sugar industry.

Labour: Labour comprises the people involved in the manufacturing process as well those who are involved in the administration of the industry. They are both skilled as well as unskilled. Large-scale industries require a large number of labourers. These industries build a township to accommodate the workers. Such industrial townships can be found in Durgapur, Jamshedpur and Bhillai.

Power: Power is needed to process the raw material. Power is transmitted to the industrial centers through power plants.

Transport: Transport plays an important factor as it links the source of the raw material to the industry and the industry to the market. Heavy industries such as iron and steel are well-connected to the market and the source of raw materials is connected by roads, railways or by navigable rivers. Close proximity to the port and the railway station is also an important factor that determine the location of an industry.

Transport links the source to the raw material

Market: Market is considered to be an important factor in determining the location of an industry. Proximity to the market is essential as it facilitates quick disposal of the product to the consumer. It helps in reducing the transport cost and helps the consumer to get things at cheaper rates. Many consumer industries are located near a market. A ready market is necessary for perishable commodities like agro-based products.

Government policies

The government plays an important role in determining the location of an industry. The government of India has set up infrastructural facilities to promote industrial growth in underdeveloped areas. It also gives certain benefits in taxes to encourage industrial growth in the backward areas. Thus, government policies play an important role in encouraging or discouraging the location pattern of industries.

Special Economic Zone

A special economic zone is an area in which business and trade laws are different from the rest of the country. The reason for the creation of special economic zones by the host country is to attract foreign manufacturing industry. At present, there are eight functional SEZs located in India.

- Santa Cruz in Maharashtra
- Kandla and Surat in Gujarat
- Vishakhapatnam in Andhra Pradesh
- Noida in Uttar Pradesh
- Kochi in Kerala
- Chennai in Tamil Nadu
- Falta in West Bengal
- Indore in Madhya Pradesh

Industrial Regions

A number of industries located close to each other form an industrial region. These are the regions where industries are concentrated due to a favourable industrial location. These are areas within which manufacturing is carried out on a large scale.

heavy industries: industries that manufacture large, heavy articles and materials in bulk

The major industrial regions of the world are:

- Eastern North America
- Western and Central Europe
- Eastern Europe
- Eastern Asia

The major industrial regions of the world are located in the temperate areas, near sea ports, where a high degree of technological proficiency is available and near the source of raw materials.

The major industrial regions of India are:

- Mumbai-Pune Industrial Region
- Bengaluru-Tamil Nadu Industrial Region
- Hugli Industrial Region
- Ahmedabad-Vadodara Industrial Region
- Chhota Nagpur Industrial Region
- Vishakhapatnam- Guntur Industrial Region
- Gurugram–Delhi–Meerut Industrial Region
- Kollam–Thiruvananthapuram Industrial Region

FactPedia

India witnessed a slow industrial growth because of British policies. Small-scale industries such as handicrafts and textiles suffered greatly during British rule. The workers were not paid adequate wages and the working conditions were not good either.

Industrial Pollution and Environmental Degradation

We have learnt that industry plays a major role in the economic growth and development of a country. Manufacturing industries cause environmental degradation as manufacturing involves a series of processes to convert the raw materials to the goods of utility. Industries cause the following types of pollution:

- Air pollution is caused by the presence of undesirable gases like sulphur dioxide, carbon monoxide and nitrogen dioxide. Smoke is also emitted by industries and the burning of fossil fuels like coal.
- Water pollution is caused by organic and inorganic industrial wastes and affluent discharge into rivers by chemical industries. Paper industries, chemical industries, textile industries, dyeing, petroleum refineries, leather industries and electroplating industries are the main causes of water pollution.
- Thermal pollution of water happens when hot water from factories and thermal power plants is discharged into rivers and ponds before being brought to normal temperature. It adversely affects aquatic life.
- Noise pollution occurs due to construction activities, machinery, different factory equipments and electrical drills. These noises cause irritation and affect the well-being of the workers. Loud noise from factories also causes hearing impairment and increases blood pressure and heartbeat.

Figure Out

How does noise affect our ears? Study the structure of the ears to understand the effects of loud noise to our ears.

Preventing Environmental Degradation

Some of the important measures to reduce environmental degradation are:

- **Control at the source:** Industries should treat the exhaust gases and the solid waste before discharging them.
- **Site selection:** The industrial site should be located far from thickly populated regions. The climatic condition and topographical features should be analyzed and studied properly before setting up the industry.
- **Afforestation:** Afforestation is intensive plantation to protect the environment and prevent further degradation. Intensive plantation in the industrial regions should be encouraged to reduce pollution.

DIY

The Bhopal Gas Tragedy which occurred on 3 December 1984 was one of the worst industrial disasters of India. Find out how the disaster took place and how it affected the environment and lives of the people. Prepare a report and a timeline to explain the course of the events.

- **Government:** As India went through a phase of industrial development, different organizations were established to deal with environmental concerns. The government of India has constituted Pollution Control Boards (PCBs) at the national and state levels. These boards have the capacity and authority to survey the industrial area to find out the amount of emission. They also have the capacity to close the industry if they do not follow government guidelines set up mainly for the protection and improvement of the environment.

Geo Connect

Japan is one of the world's leading nations in industrial development. The country experienced a rapid industrial growth after the Second World War. The industrial development of Japan is mainly due to Keiretsu which is a Japanese term that literally means a 'group of enterprises'. It is a well-knit group of manufacturers, suppliers, distributors and banks, which forms the backbone of the Japanese manufacturing industry. The major industries are petrochemicals, pharmaceuticals, textile, aerospace, shipbuilding and food processing.

In a Nutshell

- Manufacturing industries play an important role in the economic development of a country.
- Industries are classified on the basis of raw material, size and ownership.
- The agro-based industry derives raw materials from agriculture whereas, the mineral-based industry derives raw materials from minerals.
- The development of industries is influenced by raw materials, labour, transport, market and government policies.
- Manufacturing industries cause environmental pollution.

Workout

A. Fill in the blanks.

1. .... is an activity involved in the production of goods.
2. ....-based industry produces furniture.
3. .... plantation in the industrial regions should be encouraged to reduce pollution.
4. .... is used to make tyres.
5. .... and .... are examples of private sector industries.

B. Choose the correct answer and fill in the blanks.

1. At present, there are .... functional SEZs located in India.
   a. six b. seven c. eight d. nine
2. Pulp and paper, pharmaceuticals, furniture and construction materials are .... industries.
   a. agro-based b. mineral-based c. forest-based d. marine-based
3. .... pollution is caused due to the presence of undesirable gases.
   a. Air b. Land c. Water d. Noise
4. .... is intensive plantation to protect the environment and prevent further degradation.
   a. Deforestation b. Afforestation
   c. Desertification d. Reforestation

C. Give reasons.

1. Proper rail and road connections are a requisite for industries.
2. Trees should be planted around large-scale industries.
3. Manufacturing industries are the backbone of any country.

D. Answer in one word.

1. Industry that processes seafood: ....
2. The process of changing raw material into a more valuable product: ....
3. A primary industry: ....

E. Answer these questions in brief.

1. Define manufacturing.
2. How can the government of a country promote its industrial growth?
3. What is an industrial region?
4. What is a Special Economic Zone?
5. What is a cottage industry?

G. Answer these questions in detail.

1. Differentiate between an agro-based and a mineral-based industries.
2. How does the availability of raw materials and labour affect the location of industries?

Across the Boundary 2

Be A Scientist

The greenhouse effect is a matter of great concern for all scientists. Our planet is getting warmer and warmer by the day due to human activities.

1. With the help of your geography, science and English teachers, make a wall magazine analyzing how waste gases from factories, power plants and cars are building up in the atmosphere and trapping too much heat in the Earth.
2. With the help of your science teacher, find out how these gases are reacting in the atmosphere and how they are affecting the environment.
3. With the help of your geography and science teachers, find out information about the environmental problems caused by the greenhouse effect.
4. With the help of your English teacher, collect different slogans to spread awareness on the importance of saving the atmosphere.
5. Compile all your data into a wall magazine and put it up on your school bulletin board for everyone to read.

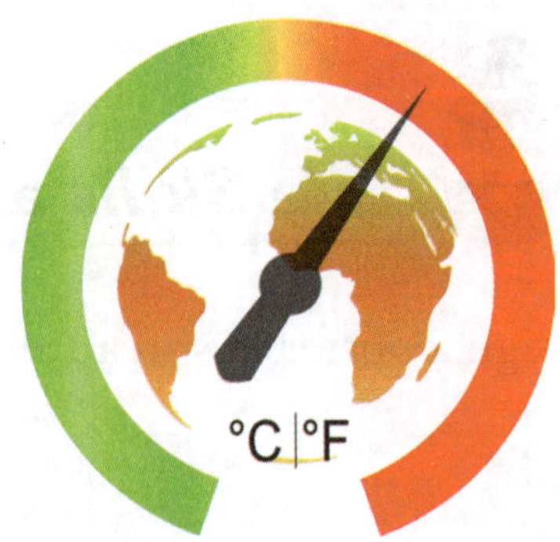

7 Energy and Power Resources

Let's learn about...

- conventional and unconventional sources of energy.
- renewable and non-renewable sources of energy.
- major hydroelectric projects of India.
- conservation of energy and power resources.

Key Terms

- renewable energy
- non-renewable energy
- conventional energy
- non-conventional energy
- hydroelectricity
- conservation of energy

Reflect

Science and technology has made our lives easier. Most of us begin our day by switching on the geyser. We iron our clothes and then eat breakfast. We go to the school by bus. Discuss with your classmates and find out what makes the geyser heat up the water and what makes the buses move.

Energy is needed in every walk of life. Imagine a day without electricity and think of the difficulties you would face. Energy is needed for lighting houses and streets, warming and cooling houses, running vehicles, running machines in factories, for household appliances to work and for cooking. We derive energy from fossil fuels. Energy is generated from fossil fuels such as coal, petroleum and natural gas. People staying in remote villages mainly use cow dung cakes, coal and firewood for cooking.

Sources of Energy

Conventional sources of energy

The conventional sources of energy include firewood, coal, petroleum, natural gas and electricity generated from water and wind. They are also known as non-renewable sources of energy. Once they have been used up, they cannot be replenished as they are available in limited quantities.

Non-conventional sources of energy

Non-conventional sources of energy are also known as alternative sources of energy. These sources of energy are mainly generated from solar energy, wind energy, geothermal energy, and biogas.

3. Write three ways in which environmental degradation caused by industries can be prevented.
4. Differentiate between private and cooperative sector industry.
5. Explain the factors that determine the location of industries.

H. Map Work

1. On an outline map of India, mark the major industrial regions of India.
2. On an outline map of the world, mark the major industrial regions of the world.

Think Box

Trace the journey of your notebook from raw material to a usable product. You can show the stages with the help of a flowchart.

Picture Study

Look at this picture and answer the questions.

1. This is a steel manufacturing plant. What type of industry is it on the basis of size and raw material?
2. How is it different from the textile industry?

Life Skills and Values

Design a poster to spread awareness about the way industries pollute the environment.

Enjoy

Prepare a PowerPoint presentation on the handloom industry of India. You can include points such as the history of the hand loom industry, conditions of artisans and how they earn their living.

Weblinks

For more information, visit
https://www.ibef.org/industry/manufacturing-sector-india.aspx
Last accessed on 31/July/2020

They are also referred to as renewable sources as they will not run out in the near future. The non-conventional sources of energy are eco-friendly. We will study about these sources in detail later in this chapter.

Sources of conventional energy

The conventional sources of energy are the chief sources of commercial energy. The major fuels used are coal, natural oil or petroleum and natural gas.

> **Figure Out**
> Talk to your grandparents about their experiences with vehicles running on steam engines. Compare them with vehicles driven by electric or diesel engines.

Coal: Coal has been used for centuries as a fuel. During the Industrial Revolution, it was used to produce steam power to run factory machineries and railway locomotives. It was the most important fuel for factories, locomotives and steamships. In India, coal is the most abundantly used fossil fuel. India is highly dependent on coal for meeting its commercial energy as well as for its domestic needs. We already know that coal is a sedimentary rock which is formed due to the compression of organic matter, mainly plants, over a long period of time. Coal exists in a variety of forms depending upon depth, time and the amount of compression. The highest quality of coal is anthracite and bituminous, whereas lignite and peat are of lower quality. Coal is a bulky fuel which reduces on burning. It is used to generate electricity in thermal power plants. It is also used in the iron and steel industry and chemical industry. Coal is an important resource today in many spheres. It is not only used as a fossil fuel but also as a raw material for many other industries.

Petroleum: Petroleum is also called mineral or natural oil. It is the main source of many products like petrol, diesel oil, kerosene, benzene, Vaseline® and paraffin wax. Petroleum is one of the most widely-used fossil fuels. It is the next major source of energy in India after coal. Petroleum provides fuel for heating, lighting, and lubricants for machinery. It has several advantages and it has the widest range of domestic as well as industrial uses. It is therefore often referred to as 'black gold'. Petroleum refineries act as a nodal industry for synthetic fibre, the fertilizer industry and numerous chemical industries. India has twelve oil refineries. The crude oil obtained from the Earth needs refining and is carried through pipelines to refineries. Mineral oil is highly inflammable in nature. It is transported through pipelines to avoid hazards. The major share of the country's production is from Mumbai High. It has the largest mineral oil deposits in India and are found in the offshore sea near Mumbai. Sagar Samrat is the oil drilling platform located off the coast of Mumbai. India imports about 70 per cent of mineral oil in order to meet its requirement of mineral oil. Ankeleshwar is one of the most important oil fields located in Gujarat. The oldest oil producing state is Assam. Digboi is one of the oldest oil fields in India.

> **FactPedia**
> The word petroleum is derived from the word *petra* meaning rock and *oleum* meaning oil. Thus, petroleum literally means 'rock oil'. It is extracted from the rocks.

Natural Gas: Natural gas is considered an environment friendly fuel because of its low carbon dioxide emissions. This gas may occur in association with petroleum. The large fields of gas often have no natural oil. In India, large reserves of natural gas have been discovered in the

nodal industry: an industry around which other small industries develop

Krishna-Godavari Basin. Along the western coast, natural gas has been discovered in the region of Mumbai High. The Andaman and Nicobar Islands also have reserves of natural gases.

Generating Electricity

We have read about the sources of energy which are also known as energy resources. Electricity is generated from these sources. They have a wide range of applications in the modern world. Electricity is mainly harnessed in two ways for commercial use—thermal electricity and hydroelectricity.

Green Earth

Find out why generation of thermal electricity is not eco-friendly.

Thermal electricity

Thermal electricity is harnessed from coal, petroleum and natural gas. These power stations use fossil fuels to generate electricity. You have already learnt that fossil fuels are non-renewable resources. There are over 310 thermal power stations in India. As thermal electricity is produced from exhaustible minerals, it is more expensive. Waste disposal is also of great concern.
The disposal of the ash generated from a coal-based thermal power plant is neither economical nor environment friendly.

Hydroelectricity

Hydroelectricity is generated by allowing the flowing water to pass over huge turbines with great force. Water is a renewable resource and can be used and reused for a long time. Thus, a hydel power plant is eco-friendly and less expensive as compared to a thermal power plant. The initial cost for the setting up of dams, power stations and transmission lines is high but the production cost of hydroelectricity is low.

Hydroelectric projects in India

Dam	**River**
Tehri dam	Bhagirathi
Koyna dam	Koyna
Srisailam	Krishna
Nathpa Jhakri	Sutlej
Sardar Sarovar Dam	Narmada
Bhakra-Nangal	Sutlej
Chamera I	Ravi
Linganamakki	Sharavathi
Indira Sagar	Narmada
Nagarjuna Sagar	Krishna
Idukki	Periyar
Salal	Chenab
Omkareshwar	Narmada
Teesta	Teesta river

Alternative Sources of Energy

Conventional sources of energy such as coal and petroleum get exhausted as they cannot be replenished once they are used. Sources of energy such as the sun, wind and tides can be used to generate energy to reduce human dependency on fossil fuels. The overutilization of fossil fuels causes serious environmental problems.

Nuclear or atomic energy

Nuclear energy is a non-conventional source of energy. It has a wide range of uses in the field of medicine. Nuclear energy is obtained from minerals such as thorium and uranium. These minerals undergo changes and release energy. Heat energy is released when the atomic structure of these minerals is altered. This heat energy in turn is used to generate electric power. There are several nuclear power stations in India. These are located in Maharashtra, Rajasthan, Tamil Nadu, Karnataka, Gujarat and Uttar Pradesh.

Solar energy

The Sun is the ultimate source of energy. It is a store house of vast inexhaustible energy. We have already learnt that the Sun radiates solar energy in the form of solar radiation. The Earth receives only a small fraction of this heat. India, being a tropical country and receiving sunlight throughout the year, is ideal for the development and use of solar energy. Solar energy is a popular source of energy in the rural and remote regions of India. In hilly regions, many houses have solar panels. Development of solar power plants reduces the dependency of rural households on less efficient fuels such as cow dung cake, firewood and coal.

We can follow some of these steps to conserve electricity.

1. Use compact florescent lamps (CFLs). They save energy.
2. During the daytime, we should switch off the lights. Using minimum electricity during the day saves electricity.
3. We should try to identify the causes of electricity wastage and carry out necessary steps to avoid this.
4. We should try to use energy efficient electrical appliances. Electrical appliances are rated for their efficiency. While buying appliances such as air conditioners and refrigerators, we must always check how energy efficient they are.
5. To conserve fossil fuels such as petrol and diesel, we can also practise carpooling instead of using individual cars.

Wind energy

Windmills have been used since time immemorial in farms for grinding grains. They are also used to generate electricity. The force of the wind is used to move the turbines and then convert it into electricity. The electricity is used for household and agricultural purposes.

India has great potential for wind energy, mainly in the coastal regions of Gujarat, Odisha, Andhra Pradesh, Maharashtra, Karnataka and Goa. India has the largest windmill in Tamil Nadu from Nagarcoil to Madurai. Jaisalmer also has windmills for the generation of electricity.

FactPedia

The Netherlands is also known as the 'land of windmills'. It is one of the leading users of wind energy in the world.

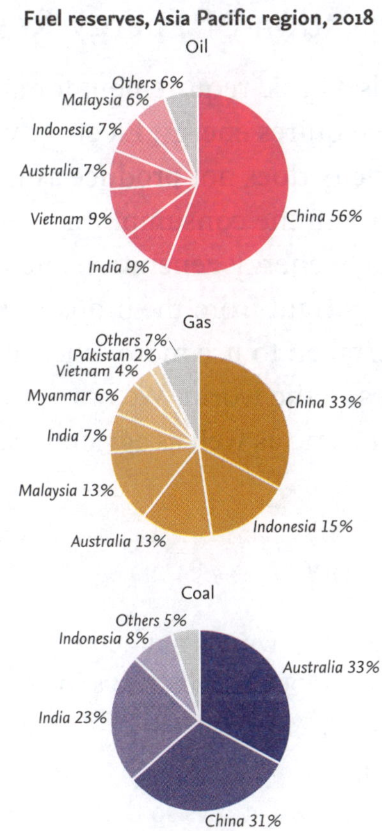

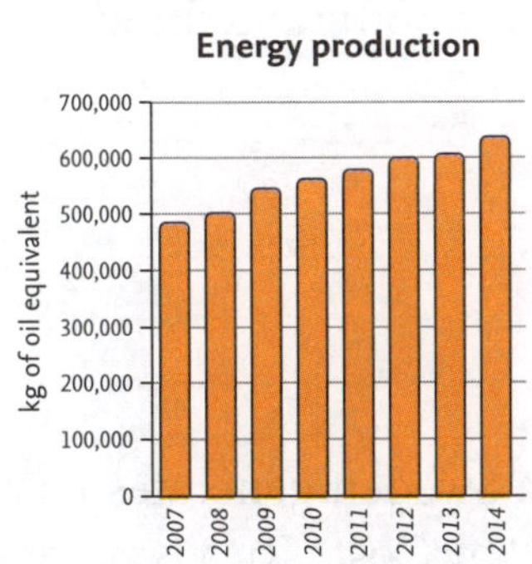

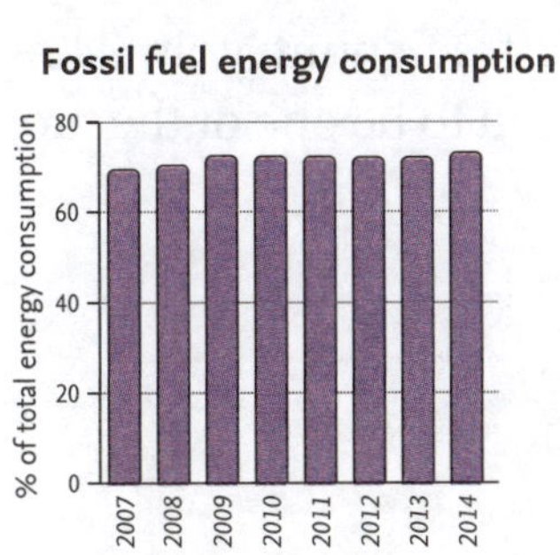

Fuel distribution and power generation in India

Conservation of Energy Resources

Energy is a basic requirement for any country's domestic as well industrial use. Every sector in the country requires energy. Electricity can be easily transported over long distances by wires. The use of electricity does not produce ash. Rapid industrialization and economic development has led to a steady rise in the consumption of energy. Therefore, there is an urgent need to develop sustainable methods of energy generation and development. Energy conservation should be practised in all spheres right from the industry to household activities. Research and development should be undertaken to use more renewable energy resources. India is one of the least energy efficient countries in the world. We have to adopt a policy to use non-conventional sources of energy for both domestic as well as agricultural use.

DIY

Make your own anemometer

Materials: pencil, pin, two straws, stapler, scissors, cone pattern, paper, tape, bottle with a narrow neck, stopwatch or watch

Steps:

1. Staple two straws so that they make the shape X. Reinforce with a tape.
2. Cut out a pattern for four cones. Color one cone red.
3. Staple one cone pattern to each straw end, so they all face the same way.
4. Curve each cone pattern to form a cone and secure with a tape.
5. Pin the centre of the X to the pencil eraser.
6. Insert the pencil in a narrow-necked bottle, so that you can hold the bottle and the anemometer will spin freely.

Geo Connect

The entire world is concerned about the depletion of fossil fuels. Sweden generates its electricity mainly from solar and wind energy. A huge amount of energy used by Costa Rica is generated from hydro, geothermal, wind and solar energy. Even Scotland generates a major chunk of its electricity from wind power. Denmark also aims to become a fossil fuel free country. It also generates its major household electricity from wind. Wind energy is considered to be one of the most promising alternative source of energy in the near future.

In a Nutshell

- Energy is required for performing everyday activities.
- Conventional sources of energy refer to the traditional sources of energy such as coal, petroleum and natural gas.

- The non-conventional sources of energy are also referred to as renewable sources of energy.
- Overuse of energy resources has caused their depletion.

Workout

A. Choose the correct answer.

1. .... is an alternative source of energy.
   a. Coal b. Petroleum c. Solar energy d. Natural gas
2. Petroleum literally means ....
   a. rock oil b. natural oil c. mineral oil d. earth oil
3. .... is known as the 'land of windmills.'
   a. Mumbai b. Kolkata c. Netherlands d. London
4. .... are used to trap solar energy.
   a. Solar cells b. Solar panels c. Solar boards d. Dry cells

B. Answer in one word.

1. The type of energy harvested from coal: ....
2. Overutilization of fossil fuels causes: ....
3. The sources of energy that do not get exhausted: ....
4. The ultimate source of energy: ....

C. Give geographical reasons for the following.

1. There is shortage of fossil fuels in the world.
2. Coal is the main source of commercial energy
3. Advancement in solar energy will have a positive impact on the environment.
4. There is an urgent need to use alternative sources of energy.

D. Answer these questions in brief.

1. What are non-renewable sources of energy?
2. State the importance of energy.
3. Explain why natural gas is considered eco-friendly.
4. Differentiate between conventional and non-conventional sources of energy.
5. What are fossil fuels?

E. Answer these questions in detail.

1. Name the different types of coal and explain the difference between them.
2. Write three ways in which we can conserve electricity.
3. How is petroleum produced in nature?
4. What are the alternative sources of energy?

Think Box

After burning, why does coal leave a residue behind but LPG does not?

Picture Study

Look at the picture and answer the questions.

1. Which source of energy is the Sun?
2. How does the consumption of solar energy help in the conservation of energy?
3. How is it different from fossil fuels?

Life Skills and Values

Find out about the electric consumption in your house and note the number of units consumed per month over a period of four months. Plot your findings on a graph and answer the following questions.

1. In which month was the consumption maximum and what may be the probable reason?
2. In which month was the consumption minimum and what may be the probable reason?

Discuss your findings with your teacher and the class.

Enjoy

Create a PowerPoint presentation with the help of your social science teacher, science teacher and your computer teacher on the theme 'Save Energy, Save Earth'. Organize a seminar and present your PowerPoint presentations in your class. Invite students from the other classes to observe and take part in the seminar.

Weblinks

For more information, visit
https://www.ibef.org/industry/power-sector-india.aspx
Last accessed on 31/July/2020

Across the Boundary 3

Become an Industrialist

You are an industrialist and want to build a food processing industry. Develop a plan about how you will set up the industry.

1. Select a product and give it a name.
2. List down the raw materials needed to make this product.
3. Analyze the other factors of production needed to manufacture your product.
4. State the mode of transport you are going to take to link the raw materials to the industry and the finished product to the market.
5. State the way in which you are going to work on environmental protection around your industrial area.
6. Prepare an area-plan with proper mathematical dimensions allocating spaces for office, the production unit and parking place for loading and unloading. This can be in the form of a sketch.
7. Choose an appropriate location for your industry.

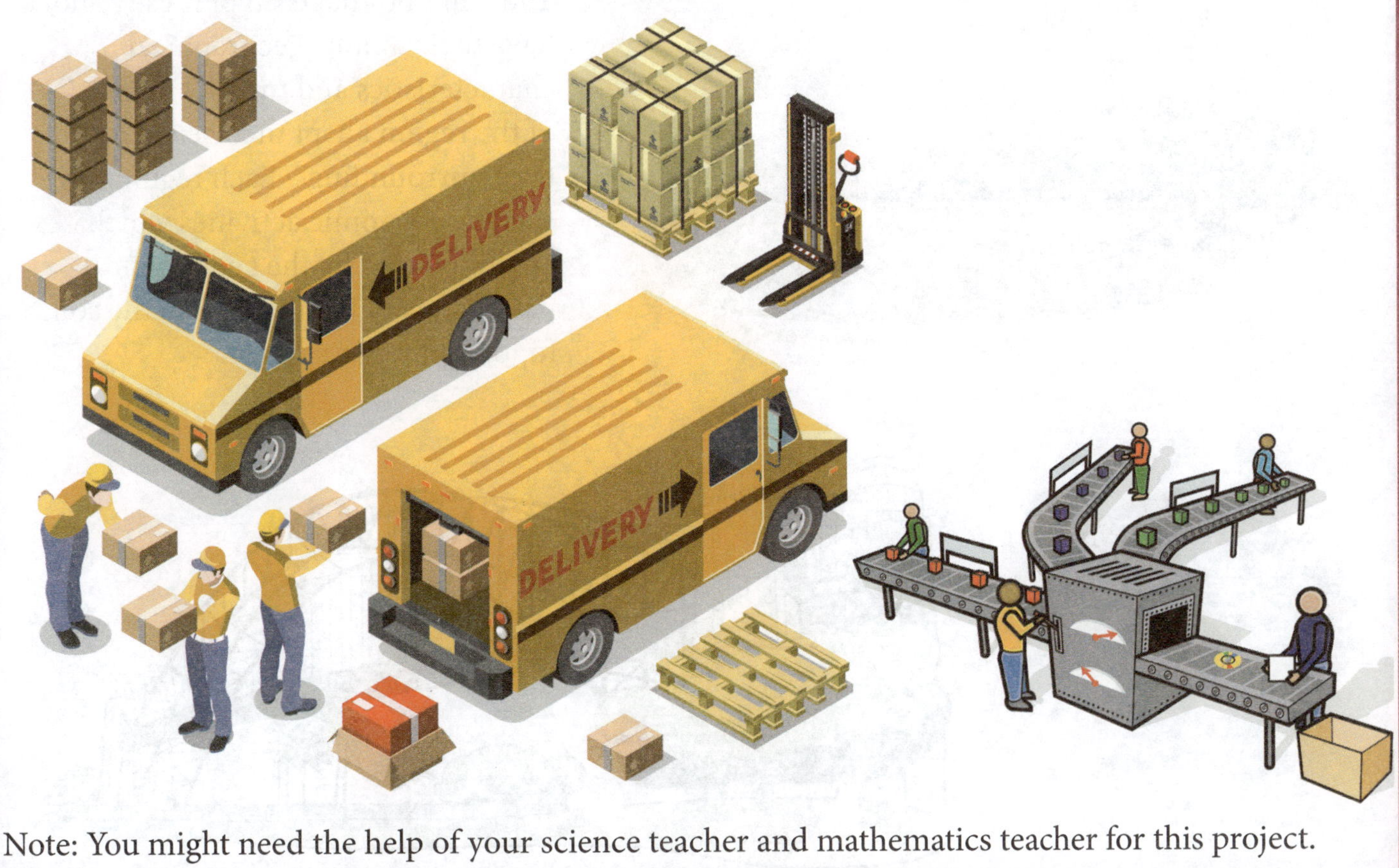

Note: You might need the help of your science teacher and mathematics teacher for this project.

Theme 4

Regional Geography

A 'region' in geography is defined as a distinct part of the Earth's surface with similar and unique geographical features. Regional geography is the branch of geography that deals with the world's regions based on the geographical set-up, environmental factors, culture and economy. Geographers divide the Earth into different regions for convenience, as it becomes easier for them to observe, analyze and explain each region. In the following chapters, you will learn about Europe, Africa, Antarctica and Australia.

★ SWITZERLAND ★

You will find that each of these regions have their unique geographical characteristics and the way people of the region adapt themselves to their surroundings. Each region has specific economic activities which are influenced by the geographical parameters of the region like the soil, topography and climate.

8 Europe

Let's learn about...

- political divisions of Europe.
- physical features of Europe.

Key Terms

- Europe
- Urals
- Caucasus

Reflect

Football is the most popular sport in this continent. It is the second smallest continent and has a rich history which includes the history of Ancient Greece, the Roman Civilization and the Renaissance amongst many others.

What continent am I? ....

Europe is a relatively small continent as compared to Asia, North America, South America and Africa with Australia being the only continent smaller. It has a considerable physical diversity and it is often referred to as a 'dynamic continent'.

EUROPE AT A GLANCE

Longitudinal extent: 25°W to 65°E
Latitudinal extent: 35°N to 72°N
Highest Elevation: Mount Elbrus, Russia
Lowest Point: The Caspian Sea
Area: 10 million sq km
Largest watershed: The Volga
Number of countries: 51
Population density: 34 people per square km

Location

Europe is bordered in the north by the Arctic Ocean, in the west by the Atlantic Ocean, and in the south by the Mediterranean Sea, the Black Sea and the Caspian Sea. In the east, Europe is bordered by the Ural Mountains and in the west, by the Atlantic Ocean. Europe is the westernmost part of the supercontinent Eurasia. The Ural and the Caucasus mountains separate Europe from Asia.

Political Divisions

Although Europe has only seven per cent of the total land area of the world, the continent has more than forty countries. Most of these countries are small in area. Presently, the European countries are grouped on the basis of geographical similarities.

- In the extreme north of Europe are Norway, Sweden, Finland, Iceland and Denmark. They are called the Scandinavian or the Nordic Countries.
- The United Kingdom and France make up Western Europe. The United Kingdom is a part of the British Isles which comprises more than a six thousand smaller isles. The United Kingdom includes the main island, Great Britain, Northern Ireland and many smaller islands.

FactPedia

The Prime Meridian passes through Greenwich, near London, from where the Greenwich Mean Time (GMT) is taken as the International Standard Time (IST).

- The Netherlands, Belgium, and Luxembourg are called the Lowland Countries. This region is also known as Benelux—'Be' for Belgium 'ne' for Netherlands and 'lux' for Luxembourg. The Netherlands is also known as Holland.
- France, UK, Ireland and the Lowland Countries are together called the West European Countries.

Figure Out

Compare the size of Europe with that of Asia.

- The Iberian Peninsula or Iberia is located on the southwest corner of Europe. This peninsula includes most of Spain and Portugal, parts of France, Andorra and the British Overseas Territory of Gibraltar.
- The Italian or the Apennine Peninsula is a region located to the south of Europe. It includes Italy, San Marino and the Vatican City. Germany, Switzerland, Austria, Poland, Hungary, Czech Republic and Slovakia make up Central Europe.
- The Balkan Peninsula is located in southeast Europe. It includes Serbia, Albania, Bosnia, Herzegovina, Bulgaria, Croatia, Greece, Montenegro, European Turkey, and former Yugoslavia and Romania. These are also called Balkan States.
- The countries located along the coast of the Baltic Sea make up Eastern Europe.
- The nine republics of Russia that are in Europe are Estonia, Latvia, Lithuania, Belarus, Ukraine, Moldova, Georgia, Armenia and Azerbaijan. Estonia, Latvia and Lithuania are called the Baltic States.

isles: islands

A B C D E F G H I J K L
D E F G H
1 2 3 4 5 6
GREENLAND
ICELAND
Reykjavik
Arctic Circle
ATLANTIC OCEAN
Norwegian Sea
Barents Sea
North Sea
NORWAY
SWEDEN
FINLAND
Oslo
Stockholm
Helsinki
Tallinn
ESTONIA
St Petersburg
RUSSIAN FEDERATION
Moscow
LATVIA
Rīga
LITHUANIA
Vilnius
RUS. FED.
Minsk
BELARUS
DENMARK
Copenhagen
IRELAND
Dublin
Belfast
Edinburgh
UNITED KINGDOM
London
Cardiff
The Hague
NETH.
Amsterdam
Brussels
BEL.
LUX.
Luxembourg
Berlin
GERMANY
Rhine
POLAND
Warsaw
Prague
CZECH REPUBLIC
SLOVAKIA
Bratislava
Vienna
AUSTRIA
Munich
Kiev
UKRAINE
Volga
Volgograd
KAZAKHSTAN
Caspian Sea
Crimea
Odesa
MOLDOVA
Chişinău
Bay of Biscay
Paris
Seine
FRANCE
Lyon
Bern
SW.
Budapest
HUNGARY
ROMANIA
Bucharest
Ljubljana
SL.
Zagreb
CROATIA
Milan
MONACO
SAN MARINO
B.H.
Sarajevo
Belgrade
SERBIA
Danube
Black Sea
GEORGIA
AZERBAIJAN
ARMENIA
AZ.
PORTUGAL
Lisbon
SPAIN
Madrid
A.
Andorra la Vella
Barcelona
ITALY
Rome
MO.
K.
Priština
Podgorica
Tirana
ALBANIA
Skopje
MAC.
BULGARIA
Sofia
İstanbul
Ankara
TURKEY
GREECE
Athens
Mediterranean Sea
Gibraltar (UK)
Valletta
MALTA
Nicosia
CYPRUS
LEBANON
SYRIA
IRAQ
ISRAEL
JORDAN
MOROCCO
ALGERIA
TUNISIA
LIBYA
EGYPT
SAUDI ARABIA
Tropic of Cancer
NIGER
CHAD
SUDAN
Country abbreviations
A. ANDORRA
B.H. BOSNIA-HERZEGOVINA
BEL. BELGIUM
K. KOSOVO
L. LIECHTENSTEIN
LUX. LUXEMBOURG
MAC. MACEDONIA (FYROM)
MO. MONTENEGRO
NETH. NETHERLANDS
RUS. FED. RUSSIAN FEDERATION
SL. SLOVENIA
SW. SWITZERLAND
Key
Countries
Capital city
Important city/town

Greenland
Greenland Sea
Spitsbergen
Edgeøya
Svalbard
Barents Sea
Novaya Zemlya
Yamal Peninsula
Obskaya Guba
Bjørnøya
Arctic Circle
Jan Mayen
Denmark Strait
ATLANTIC OCEAN
North Cape
Ostrov Kolguyev
Iceland
Snæfell 1833
Norwegian Sea
Inarijärvi
Lofoten
Lappland
Kola Peninsula
M. Kanin
Pechora
Usa
Gora Narodnaya 1894
Ural Mountains
Kemi
White Sea
Mezen
Scandinavia
Lule
Ume
Gulf of Bothnia
Northern Dvina
Vychegda
Kama
Faroe Islands
Indals
Lake Onega
Shetland Islands
Åland Islands
Lake Ladoga
Orkney Islands
Outer Hebrides
Vänern
Mälaren
Gulf of Finland
Rybinskoye Vodokhranilishche
Ben Nevis 1344
Malin Head
North Sea
Skagerrak
Vättern
Lake Peipus
Gulf of Riga
Gotland
Volga
Kuybyshevskoye Vodokhranilishche
British Isles
Pennines
Galway Bay
Shannon
Irish Sea
Öland
Zealand
Fyn
Bornholm
Baltic Sea
North European Plain
Valdai Hills
Volga Uplands
Cape Clear
Ireland
Great Britain
Snowdon 1085
Central Russian Upland
Elbe
Weser
Oder
Vistula
Pripet Marshes
Dnieper
Land's End
Isles of Scilly
Thames
Strait of Dover
Maas
Rhine
Taunus
Warta
Bug
English Channel
Channel Is
Seine
Marne
Moselle
Sudety
Kyyivs'ke Vodoskhovyshche
Don
Ural
Tsimlyanskoye Vodokhranilishche
Brittany
Loire
Bay of Biscay
Vosges
Danube
Inn
Carpathian Mts
Dniester
Volga
Caspian Sea
Saône
Jura
Grossglockner 3798
Lake Balaton
Tisza
Dnieper
Sea of Azov
Stavropol'skaya Vozvyshennost'
Mt Dore 1885
L. Geneva
Mt Blanc 4810
Alps
Hungarian Plain
Crimea
El'brus 5642
Cape Finisterre
Dordogne
Massif Central
Matterhorn 4478
Po
Mureș
Transylvanian Alps
Caucasus
Gulf of Gascony
Cantabrian Mts
Rhône
Sava
Dinaric Alps
Danube
Douro
Duero
Pyrenees
Aneto 3404
Gulf of Lions
Gulf of Genoa
Apennines
Adriatic Sea
Morava
Balkan Mts
Black Sea
Ebro
Corsica
Rhodope Mts
Sea of Marmara
Kelkit
Kızılırmak
Mount Ararat 5165
Tagus
Sierra Morena
Guadalquivir
Balearic Is
Sardinia
Vesuvius 1281
Lake Van
Tigris
Lake Urmia
Cabo de São Vicente
Sierra Nevada
Minorca
Majorca
Ibiza
Tyrrhenian Sea
Pindus Mts
Aegean Sea
Lake Tuz
Strait of Gibraltar
Mediterranean Sea
Ionian Sea
Taurus Mts
Sicily
Mt Etna 3323
C. Passero
Dodecanese
Euphrates
Atlas Mountains
Atlas Saharien
Chott Melrhir
Crete
Cyprus
Mt Troödos 1951
Gulf of Gabès
Chott el Jerid
ASIA
Dead Sea
Nile Delta
Gulf of Sirte
Al Jabal al Akhdar
Suez Canal
Sinai
An Nafūd
Libyan Plateau
Qattâra Depression
Libyan Desert
Gulf of Suez
Eastern Desert
Nile
Red Sea
AFRICA
Tropic of Cancer
Sahara
Lake Nasser
Plateau du Djado
Tibesti
Key
Relief and physical features
Relief metres
5000
3000
2000
1000
500
200
sea level
under sea level
0
200
4000
6000
Permanent ice (ice cap or glacier)

Physical Features

Europe can be divided into four major physical divisions:

- The Northern Highlands
- The Central Uplands
- The North European Plains
- The Alpine Mountain System

The Northern Highlands

The Northern Highlands, also called Western Uplands, extend across Finland, Norway, Scotland and Sweden. This region extends from the Ural Mountains to the Atlantic Ocean. This land is made up of sedimentary, metamorphic and igneous rocks that have been subjected to weathering and glacial erosion. The denudation causes the wearing down of the mountains that causes them to recede. Therefore, most of the peaks in this region are low with gentle slopes. The northern part of the Northern Highlands is called the Fennoscandia.

The Northern Highlands of Europe consist of the following features:

- Urals form the conventional boundary between Europe and Asia. They are a low mountain range.
- The Scandinavian mountains extend across the Scandinavian Peninsula which includes Sweden, Norway and Finland. Due to prolonged glacial erosional activity, a number of distinct physical features like lakes, fjords and marshlands were formed. The coastline along Norway is highly indented and is full of fjords penetrating the land.

Ural Mountains, Russia

- The Pennines are a range of mountains in Northern England. They are made up of old crystalline rocks. The mountains in this region are glacier eroded thus, they are marked with U-shaped valleys.
- The highland around the Baltic Sea is known as the Baltic Shield. This region has an undulating surface and is made up of igneous and metamorphic rocks.

The North European Plains

The North European Plain extends from the Atlantic coast in west to the Ural Mountains in the east. Its westward extension are the British Isles. The North European Plains cover about half of Europe. It includes parts of France, Belgium, the Netherlands, Germany, Denmark, Poland, the Baltic states and Belarus. The plain is broadest in the eastern part and narrows down towards the west.

- The Russian Plain is also called the East European Plain. Most of the northern Russian Plain is covered with ice. The southern part of the plain is covered with loess, which is a wind-blown sediment deposited by the cold winds blowing from the north.

- The Western and mid-European plains are made of deposits of alluvium brought down by the rivers. This region extends from the Pripet or Pripyat marshes to England. A major part of the region is covered by sedimentary layers making it fertile which is excellent for agriculture. It is the most densely populated part of Europe. This region is drained by a large number of navigable rivers such as the Rhine, Seine, Don, Volga, Danube, and Dnieper.

The Central Uplands

These Central Uplands lie between the North European Plains and the Alpine Mountains. The mountains are low in altitude and their height does not exceed 1600 m above the mean sea level. The region includes western France and Belgium, southern Germany, the Czech Republic, and parts of northern Switzerland and Austria.

This region consists of a system of highlands and plateaus. Geologists believe that they are broken remains of an ancient mountain system called the Hercynian System.

This Central Uplands consists of the following plateaus:

- The Meseta Central in Spain
- The Massif-Central and the Vosges in France
- The Ore and Sudeten in the Czech Republic
- The Black Forest and Taunus in Germany
- The Ardennes in Belgium
- The Bohemian Massif in Czech Republic

Limagne, Massif-Central, France

The Alpine Mountain System

The Alpine region comprises a series of young fold mountains. These mountains were formed during the recent geological time period. They are also known as the 'rooftop of Europe'. The Alpine Mountain System comprises seven of Europe's longest and highest mountain ranges:

- The Alps are amongst the highest mountain chains in Europe. They form a 1,200-km long and 200-km wide crescent across the European countries of France, Italy, Switzerland, Germany, Austria, Slovenia, Croatia, Bosnia, Serbia and Herzegovina, Montenegro, Serbia and Albania. Mont Blanc, the highest summit in Europe, is part of this mountain chain.

Mont Blanc

- The Pyrenees stretch from the Mediterranean Sea to the Atlantic Ocean. They are the smallest mountain range of the Alpine system. They form the natural boundary between Spain and France.

Hercynian System: the mountain system which is believed to have formed during the formation of the supercontinent Pangaea

- The Apennines form the backbone of Italy. Several peaks rise above 2,000 m, the highest being Corno Grande (2,912 m). Europe's most southerly glacier—the Calderone—is also located here. Many landforms, such as hollows, caves, underground water channels and deep gorges create a dramatically beautiful landscape of gentle peaks and vast alpine plateaus in the region.
- The Scandes are the oldest mountains in the Alpine Region. They extend 1,400 km down the spine of Scandinavia from the northernmost parts of Finland to southern Sweden and Norway. Europe's largest mountain plateau, the Hardangervidda is located here.
- The Carpathians are the youngest and most easterly of the mountains in the Alpine Region. They form an arc across Central and Eastern Europe making them the second longest mountain range in Europe. They extend from Slovakia to Romania. The range is twice as narrow as the Alps and the peaks are half as high. The outer slopes are made up of sandstone and shale while the interior contains a chain of volcanic mountains. The foothills are dominated by oaks and beech forests prevail at mid-altitude.
- The Balkan mountain range lies in the centre of Bulgaria. Although not physically connected, it forms a continuation of the Carpathians. The range extends through the middle of Bulgaria, dividing the country into two parts as it extends 560 km towards the Black Sea.
- The Rhodope Mountains stretch across the border into Greece, but only the Bulgarian part of the range is included in the Alpine Region. The Pirin Mountain is the most typically alpine in character. It has many snow-capped peaks, green lakes and numerous beautiful glacial valleys and cirques at high altitude.

Rivers

Several important rivers flow through Europe. These are:

- **Danube:** The river Danube originates in the Black Forest region of Germany. It flows across Central Europe through Austria, Hungary, Croatia and Yugoslavia.
- **Dnieper:** The Dnieper originates in the southwestern Russian Federation. It flows southwards through Belarus and Ukraine into the Black Sea.
- **Don:** The river Don originates near Moscow. It flows southeasterly towards the river Volga and then flows westwards abruptly.
- **Elbe:** The river Elbe originates in the Czech Republic and flows northwards through Germany.
- **Loire:** The river Loire is the longest river in France. It originates in the foothills of the Massif Central and flows north and west across the mainland of France.
- **Oder:** The Oder originates in the eastern Czech Republic. It flows west and north through Poland.

DIY

Make a list of ten UNESCO World Heritage sites in Europe. Discuss how they impact the tourism industry of Europe.

cirques: a semicircular, steep sided hollow on a mountainside formed by glacial erosion

- **Po:** The Po is Italy's longest river. It originates in the Alps. The Po flows west and north through northern Italy before flowing into the Adriatic Sea.
- **Rhine:** The Rhine originates in the Swiss Alps. It flows westwards forming Switzerland's northeastern border with Germany, then flows north through western Germany forming a part of the country's border with France. It finally enters the Netherlands and flows into the North Sea.

Rhine, Basel, Switzerland

- **Rhone:** The river Rhone originates in the Swiss Alps. It flows through Switzerland and France. The Rhone is the only major river that flows directly into the Mediterranean Sea.
- **Shannon:** The Shannon is the longest river in Ireland. It starts in northwestern Ireland near the foothills of Tiltinbane Mountain.
- **Volga:** The Volga is the longest river in Europe. It rises in the Valdai Hills northwest of Moscow. The Volga has around 200 tributaries most of which join it on its left bank.

Many freshwater lakes are found in Europe. They are mainly located in the northern part of Europe. These lakes were formed because of glaciation during the Ice Age. Lake Ladoga in Russia is the largest freshwater lake in Europe. Other famous lakes include Onega in Russia and Geneva in Switzerland. There are many lakes in Finland. It is known as the 'land of lakes'. It is believed that these lakes were formed after the Ice Age when water from the melting snow was left behind in the depressions carved out by glaciers.

Geo Connect

The Rocky Mountains or the Rockies of North America are a fold mountain range. Mount Elbert, which is the highest peak of the range, is located in Colorado. These mountains are geographically significant because the mearging point of the continental divide of the Americas is located in these mountains. The two divides meet at the Triple Divide Peak of the Lewis Range of the Rockies.

In a Nutshell

- Europe is one of the smallest continents. It is surrounded by the Arctic Ocean in the north and the Mediterranean Sea and the Black Sea in the south.
- The continent has four major physical divisions namely, the Northern Mountains, the Central European Plains, the Southern Plateau and the Highlands, and the Alpine Mountain System.
- There are many important rivers and lakes in Europe.

Workout

A. Fill in the blanks.

1. Europe is the .... smallest continent.
2. The .... and .... separate Europe and Asia.
3. Europe is surrounded by the .... in the north, the .... in the west and the .... and .... in the south.
4. .... is the natural boundary between Spain and France.

B. Choose the correct answer and fill in the blanks.

1. .... is the smallest continent in the world.
   a. Australia b. India
   c. Antarctica d. Europe
2. The .... are located in the Northern Highlands.
   a. Sierra Montana and the Alps b. Himalayas and the Karakoram
   c. Urals and the Scandinavian mountains d. Appalachians and Rockies
3. The Pyrenees stretch from the Mediterranean Sea to the ....
   a. Pacific Ocean b. Atlantic Ocean
   c. Indian Ocean d. Southern Ocean
4. The .... is the lowest point of Europe.
   a. Black Sea b. Dead Sea
   c. The Death Valley d. Caspian Sea

C. Answer in one word.

1. Europe and Asia combined into one region: ....
2. A chain of young fold mountains in Europe: ....
3. The highest mountain peak in Europe: ....
4. The peninsula lying between the Mediterranean and the Black Sea: ....
5. The backbone of Italy: ....

D. Answer these questions in brief.

1. Name the Benelux nations.
2. Name the main physical divisions of Europe.
3. Which is the largest freshwater lake of Europe?
4. What is the Baltic Shield?
5. What are fjords?

E. Answer these questions in detail.

1. Write a shot note on the Scandinavian countries.
2. Describe the main mountain ranges of the Alpine Mountain System.
3. Describe the main features of the Western Highlands of Europe.
4. Write a short note on the major rivers of Europe.

F. Map Work

On an outline map of Europe, mark the following:

1. The Volga
2. The Urals
3. The Caspian Sea
4. The Balkan Shield
5. Mount Blanc

Think Box

The Europeans made colonies in nations that were much larger than their country. Find out the geographical and economic reasons to expand their country.

Picture Study

Look at the picture and answer the questions.

1. This is a picture of a mountain of Europe. It is a young fold mountain. Name the mountain range.
2. Name the countries through which it extends.
3. Name its highest peak.

Life Skills and Values

Football is the most popular game of Europe. Find out the names of any five football clubs in Europe. Discuss what we can learn from the game of football.

Enjoy

Make a fact file of the rivers of Europe. The European rivers can be grouped into three categories:

1. Rivers in the east
2. Rivers in the west
3. Rivers in the Scandinavian Highlands

Weblinks

For more information, visit
https://www.kullabs.com/classes/subjects/units/lessons/notes/note-detail/727
Last accessed on 31/July/2020

9 Tourism in Switzerland

Let's learn about...

- the geography of Switzerland.
- factors that lead to tourism in Switzerland.
- eco-tourism.

Key Terms

- Switzerland
- tourism
- Swiss Alps

Reflect

Can you name the land of the best cheeses, watches and chocolates?

Switzerland is famous for its alpine passes which are important pathways between the northern and southern parts of Europe. This small country located in the heart of Western Europe is not only the land of Alps with some of the highest mountains in Europe but also has plateaus and lakes. Switzerland is known as the birthplace of modern skiing, mountaineering and different types of winter sports and recreational activities. The spectacular natural beauty of Switzerland has attracted tourists from all around the world.

The Matterhorn at sunset

Switzerland: Art and Literature

Switzerland has made some of the most impressive contributions to the fields of art and literature. Some of the most famous writers such as James Joyce, Voltaire and Thomas Mann lived in Switzerland. Henri Dunant, the founder of the International Committee of Red Cross and the World's Young Men Christian Association was from Switzerland. He also won the first ever Nobel Peace Prize in 1901. Perhaps, the most recognizable contribution to literature by a Swiss writer is *Heidi* which was written by Johanna Spyri.

The Reichenbach Falls, that have been mentioned in Sir Author Conan Doyle's *Sherlock Holmes* series of books, have made the place a famous tourist site. A memorial plate to commemorate this mention in the famous book series has been placed at the Reichenbach Falls. A Sherlock Holmes Museum is also located in the nearby town of Meiringen. The romantic poets and writers of the 19th century such as Lord Byron and Percy Shelly spent considerable time by the Lake Geneva and wrote some of the most famous poetry of the English language.

Swiss National Park

The Swiss National Park was founded on 1 August 1914. It was one of the earliest national parks in Europe. It is located in the Western Rhaetian Alps in eastern Switzerland. It is a favourite destination for children. The strict conservation of nature has preserved the biodiversity of the national park.

Tourism

Jura Mountains

The Alps have been the hallmark of Switzerland's successful tourism industry for more than a century. Without tourists, many Alpine areas would not be economically viable. In some places, over 80 per cent of jobs depend on them. The Alpine area as a whole receives 100 million visitors every year. With thousands of miles of hiking and biking trails, Switzerland is a paradise for adventurers. Mountain resorts make Switzerland the top adventure destination in Europe and one of the best in the world. Switzerland has a highly-developed tourism infrastructure, especially in the mountainous regions. The main concentration of hotels is in Grisons and Valais cantons, and in eastern Switzerland. Travel and tourism have given rise to many other sectors such as food and beverage industries.

The main factors that make Switzerland an ideal tourist location are:

Landscape

Switzerland has a unique geographical location with beautiful lakes, the Jura Mountains and the Swiss Alps. The landscape in these regions is spectacular and attracts a large number of tourists.

Lakes:

- One of the largest lakes in Europe, Lake Geneva, is located in Switzerland. It is crescent-shaped with the horns pointing south. The lake lies on the course of the Rhone. The beauty of the lake has been celebrated by tourists for years.
- Lake Lucerne is another beautiful lake which is located along the picturesque city of Lucerne.
- Lake Constance is a lake on the river Rhine at the northern foothills of the Alps. It consists of three parts—the upper lake, the lower lake and the part connecting the stretch of the Rhine. This part of the lake also lies in Germany and Austria.
- Lake Oeschinensee, a beautiful lake nestled within the Oeschinen valley just a few miles from Kandersteg, is a calm, isolated alpine lake. This lake is a UNESCO World heritage site.

Waterfalls:

Waterfalls makes the landscape of Switzerland the most visually stunning in Europe. The most famous waterfall is the Rhine located on the High Rhine on the border of Switzerland and Zurich. Geologists believe that this waterfall was formed during the last Ice Age. The Reichenbach Falls are a series of waterfalls on the Reichenbach stream in Bernese Oberland.

Climate

The climate of Switzerland is ideal for winter sports as well as summer tourism. Tourists love the mild climate and adventure lovers have a pleasant time indulging in a variety of winter sports like skiing, cycling and hiking. Diversity of climate is experienced in Switzerland. In regions with lower altitude, the weather is generally moderate. On the plateau, freezing temperatures generally occur from the month of December to early March. The higher elevation of the Jura hills and the Alps have low temperature and in the higher altitude of the Alps, glaciers are found. The foothills of the Jura hills experience more precipitation. Switzerland experiences both maritime climate and tundra climate. The temperature ranges from Arctic to Mediterranean-type. The southern part of Switzerland experiences a Mediterranean-type of climate because of its proximity to the Mediterranean Sea. The winters are milder in this part of the country as compared to the northern part.

The climate of Switzerland is characterized by special features like:

- Snowfall during spring
- A cold snap in June
- Indian autumn in summer

The best time to visit Switzerland is from May to September when the weather is mild and sunny.

Infrastructure: Tourism is an important industry for growth and employment in Switzerland. This is supported by efficient hospitality services such as hotels and tourist lodges. Development of human capital is essential for the sustainable growth of the tourism industry. Tourism schools are being established to develop human capital for supporting tourism. This development in turn gives impetus to the tourism industry.

Zurich, Switzerland

Government policy: The Swiss government plays a very active role in creating, maintaining and promoting tourism. It promotes and encourages research and development in the field of tourism. The Swiss Tourism Awards, introduced by the Swiss government, aims to reward innovative tourism projects. The government has also developed improved information, advice and booking arrangements for tourists from all around the world.

Travel and eco-tourism: Switzerland is very clean and green despite the massive flow of tourists each year. The people are very sensitive towards the environment and they protect it as a part of their community service. Volunteers regularly clean the landscape and remove the garbage that careless and insensitive tourists leave behind.

Impact of Tourism

The Alpine environment is fragile and under stress because of human activities and environmental issues. In recent years, snow has been less dependable, which is detrimental for the hotel industry. Skiers and snowboarders often unintentionally infringe on wildlife habitats.

Swiss tourism depends on the country side and the scenery but the challenge is to maintain a balance between developing the country side as a tourist spot by not damaging the environment. Therefore, the Swiss tourism department has to improve the quality of tourism and at the same time reduce the harm caused to the environment. The genuine innovation of Swiss tourism talk is the need for compatibility between the economic, the social and the environmental concerns. Sustainable tourism is one of the landmarks of this country.

Geo Connect

The Kashmir Valley is known as the 'Switzerland of India'. It is one of the most beautiful tourist destinations in India. It is said to be a paradise on the Earth. The main attraction of the Kashmir Valley is its spectacular gardens and Dal Lake. Staying in the houseboat along the river Jhelum and on Dal Lake is a special attraction for tourists. The meadow of Pahalgam is known as the 'Valley of Shepherds'. Leh and Ladakh are other spectacular regions with amazing landscapes.

impetus: something that makes a process or activity happen or happen more quickly

In a Nutshell

- Switzerland is a spectacular tourist destination.
- The geographical location and the climate makes this the most important tourist destination in the world.
- The government promotes tourism but makes laws to preserve the environment as well.
- The tourism industry is one of the most flourishing industries in Switzerland.

Workout

A. Fill in the blanks.

1. Switzerland is located in the heart of Western ....
2. Travel and tourism have given rise to many other sectors such as .... and .... industries.
3. The .... is a special climatic feature that attracts tourists to Switzerland.
4. The Alpine environment is fragile and under stress because of human activities and .... issues.

B. Choose the correct answer.

1. .... in Switzerland is one of the largest lakes in Europe.
   a. Lake Geneva   b. Lake Thun   c. Lake Constance   d. Lake Morat
2. .... is a major economic activity in Switzerland.
   a. Lumbering   b. Agriculture   c. Tourism   d. Mining
3. The Reichenbach falls are located on the ....
   a. Volga   b. Bernese Oberland   c. Both a and b   d. None of the above

C. Answer these questions in brief.

1. Describe how the climate of Switzerland influences tourism.
2. How do the people of Switzerland keep their environment clean despite the massive flow of tourism every year?

D. Answer these questions in detail.

1. Write a short note on the factors that led to tourism in Switzerland.
2. Describe the landscape of Switzerland.
3. Write a short note about the lakes and waterfall found in Switzerland.

E. Map Work

On an outline map of Switzerland, mark the following:

1. Lake Geneva   2. Zurich   3. The Alps   4. Matterhorn   5. River Rhine

Think Box

Find out the names of popular skiing and mountain climbing places in Switzerland.

Picture Study

Look at the picture and answer the questions.

1. This is the largest freshwater lake in Central Europe. Name it.
2. Name the country which shares this lake along with Switzerland.
3. Name a lake that lies wholly in Switzerland.

Life Skills and Values

India has many beautiful sites that are important tourist centres. Make a poster with a slogan to protect the environment of these places.

Enjoy

Choose any location in Europe such as the Netherlands or Italy and develop a brochure for the tourists naming the important places to visit. Provide information on transport and communication, which will be helpful for the people who visit.

Weblinks

For more information, visit
https://www.myswitzerland.com/en-in/
Last accessed on 31/July/2020

10 Antarctica

Let's learn about...

- the location of Antarctica.
- the physical divisions of Antarctica.
- the climate and vegetation of Antarctica.

Key Terms

- Antarctica
- ice sheets
- ice shelf
- Antarctic Treaty

Reflect

I am the land of penguins. I am covered with a white sheet of ice and an interesting land for scientists from all over the world.

Can you name me? ....

Location

Antarctica is the Earth's fifth-largest continent. It is located in the Antarctic Circle, a region around the South Pole. It is surrounded by the Indian Ocean, the Atlantic Ocean and the Pacific Ocean, the southern margins form the Southern Ocean. Antarctica is a unique continent. It is covered entirely with ice, 2000 meters thick, and does not have any native population. Antarctica does not have any countries, although several nations claim different parts of it. This continent is the coldest, windiest and the remotest part of the world. The Antarctic ice cap stores the largest reserve of freshwater in the world.

The Discovery of Antarctica

During the 16th century, people thought Antarctica was a region called Terra Australis, which is a continent believed to have existed based on the theory that continental land in the Northern Hemisphere should be balanced by land in the Southern Hemisphere. In 1773, Captain James Cook and his crew crossed the Antarctic Circle for the first time but only discovered a few islands but not the continent's mainland. Since 1820, many expeditions have been taken to Antarctica. Fabian Gottlieb von Bellingshausen and Mikhail Lazarev of Russia, Edward Bransfield of Britain,

native: existing naturally in a place

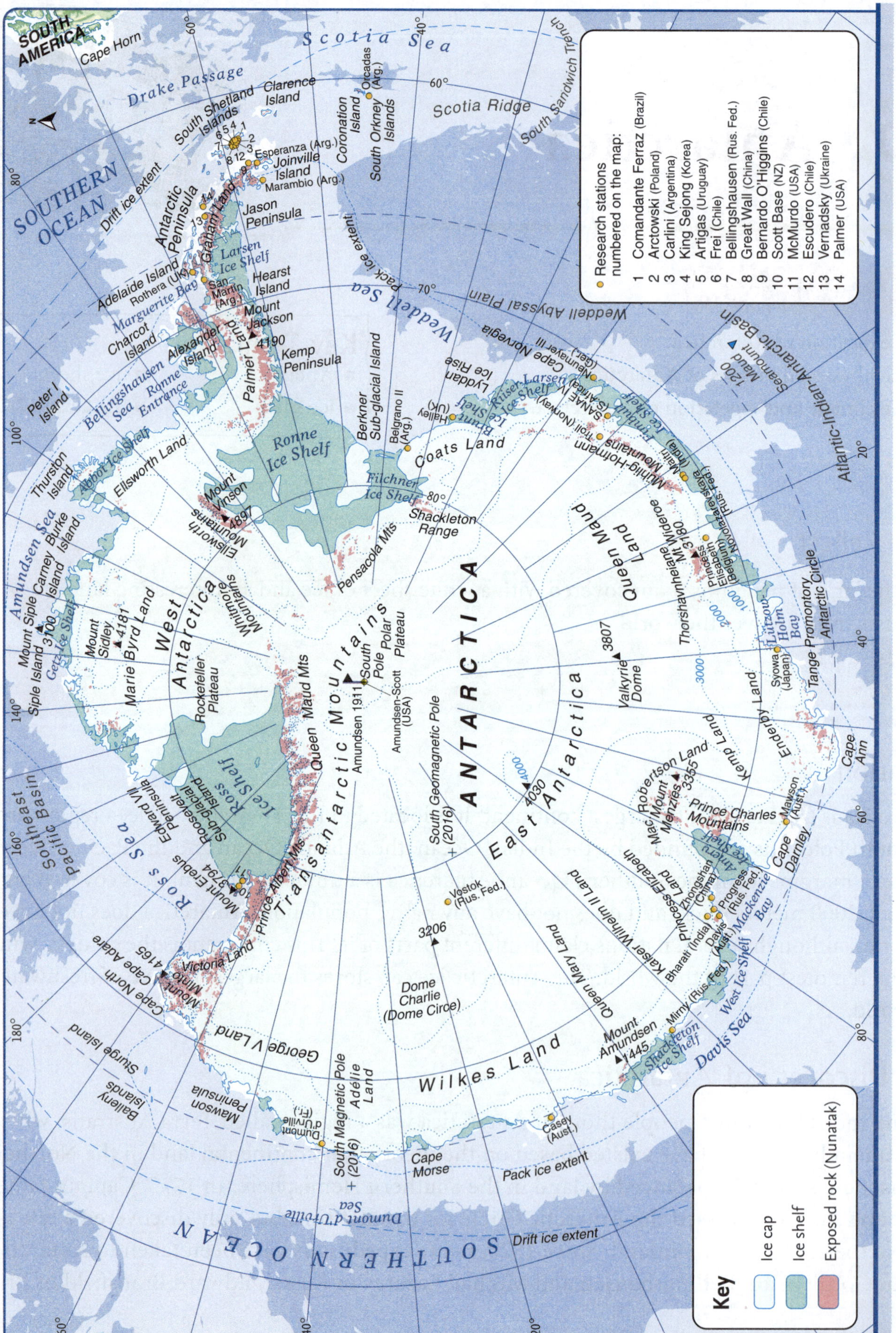

Antarctica: Physical

and Nathanial Palmer of the United States participated in expeditions to explore Antarctica. The 'heroic age' of the Antarctic exploration gathered its momentum from the lecture of John Murray at the Royal Geographic Society of London. He advocated that the research on the Antarctica will resolve a few geographical questions and queries related to the south pole of the Earth. This lead to a series of expeditions for the Antarctic exploration at the end of the 19th century and closed with Ernest Shackleton's Imperial Trans-Antarctic Expedition in 1917. Richard Evelyn Byrd of the US Navy first flew to the South Pole to study the interiors of the Antarctic.

In the recent years, due to the growing interest in the environment of the Earth and its atmosphere, the study of Antarctica has gained significance. We have read about the depletion of the ozone layer in the previous chapters. Antarctica was the place were the ozone hole was discovered.

Physical Features

Antarctica literally means 'opposite the Arctic'. It is almost circular in shape with the tip of the Antarctic peninsula extending northwards towards South America. The continent is almost entirely covered by a single ice sheet, the largest in the world, called the Antarctic Ice Sheet. On the coasts of Antarctica are the massive floating sheets of ice that are connected to the mainland. The Ross Ice Shelf and the Ronne Ice Shelf are the two major ice shelves of Antarctica.

The Transantarctic Mountains near the Ross Sea

The Transantarctic Mountains divide Antarctica into Greater Antarctica or East Antarctica, and Lesser Antarctica or West Antarctica.

Figure Out

In Antarctica, the little precipitation that occurs does not evaporate, it rather builds up over years to form the enormously thick ice sheets. Why do you think the rate of evaporation is so low in Antarctica?

- The Greater Antarctica, as the name suggests, constitutes the majority of Antarctica. It is made up of older, igneous and metamorphic rocks.
- The Lesser Antarctica or West Antarctica is a series of frozen islands. It is made up of a huge peninsula and

FactPedia

The nunatak is an exposed, rocky outcrop of a ridge or a mountain, which is not covered by ice or snow mostly found on the Transantarctic Mountains. They are home to a large number of birds such as snow petrels.

archipelago of mountainous islands. Many of these islands are volcanic and have huge glaciers. The region is made up of younger, volcanic sedimentary rocks. Mt. Erebus is an active volcano found here.

Mount Erebus

Southern or Antarctic Ocean

The Southern Ocean, or the Antarctic Ocean, comprises the southern portions of the Pacific, the Atlantic and the Indian oceans. The narrow portion of the Southern Ocean between the Antarctic Peninsula and South America is called the Drake Passage. The Southern Ocean has many seas such as the Bellingshausen Sea and the Amundsen Sea.

Climate

We know that Antarctica is one of the largest reserves of freshwater in the world. However, Antarctica is considered to be a cold desert as it experiences little to no rain. Precipitation is always in the form of snow. The interior region of the continent receives only 50 to 100 mm of snow every year. The coastal regions receive more precipitation which is around 200 mm annually. In the Antarctic peninsula, the climate is comparatively warmer with temperatures above freezing point during the summer months.

In Antarctica, the summer season lasts from October to February and the remaining months are the winter season. During the summers, the average temperature stays just below the freezing point. Antarctica experiences blizzards. The winds pick up snow from the ground and blow creating an illusion of a white blanket.

- There are three climatic regions in Antarctica—the coastal region, the interiors and the Antarctic peninsula region.
- The climate is comparatively milder with high precipitation rates, mostly in the form of snow, in the coastal region.
- The interiors of Antarctica are extremely cold with little snowfall.
- The climate is comparatively warmer and wetter, above freezing temperatures, during the summer months in the Antarctic peninsular region.

Flora and Fauna

Antarctica is almost devoid of any plant and animal life. The only vegetation—restricted to the northern and the coastal regions—is in the form of lichens, mosses and algae. The oceans surrounding Antarctica are, however, extremely diverse and swarming with marine life. Different kinds of fish and marine mammals live in these oceans. Krill, a tiny marine creature, thrives in the waters around Antarctica. Diverse species of the whale such as blue, fin, humpback, right, minke, sei and sperm whales are found in a large number in Antarctica. The leopard seal is also found in the coastal regions. It is an aggressive predator. Penguins are the most common birds found in Antarctica. They are fast swimmers. The largest penguin species is the emperor penguin.

Penguins

A leopard seal

Population

Antarctica does not have any native or indigenous population. It was discovered in the 19th century and little was known about this continent till then. It is known as the 'land of scientists'. The only form of human habitation exists at the various science research stations. The freezing weather is excellent for studying penguins, fish, global warming and climatology. Scientists drill in for ice core which can provide an insight into the geological and climatological history of the region over thousands of years. Observant satellites, with their penetrating and investigating radar and lasers, sail over the continent allowing scientists to peer beneath the thick ice cover.

The Antarctic Treaty

The Antarctic Treaty was signed in 1959 with the objective of protecting the environment of Antarctica. It allows the nations of the world to carry out scientific research and prohibits the establishment of any military bases, testing of weapons or disposing of radioactive waste. There are forty scientific research stations from different countries in Antarctica. This treaty was signed in Washington by twelve countries during the International Geophysical Year and came into force in 1961.

India In Antarctica

In December 1981, Syed Zahoor Qasim, an Indian marine biologist, led an expedition to Antarctica. Qasim and his team sailed onboard HMS Endurance and set up Dakshin Gangotri, an unmanned scientific base station. Along with Bharati and Maitri, it forms the India's Antarctic research facility.

International Geophysical Year: an international project in which scientists from all developed nations worked together to conduct research on the earth sciences

Workout

A. Fill in the blanks.

1. Antarctica is the .... largest continent in the world.
2. The Southern Ocean consists of the southern portions of the ...., ... and the .... oceans.
3. People thought Antarctica was a region called .... in the 16th century.
4. The summer season in Antarctica lasts from .... to ....

B. Choose the correct answers and fill in the blanks.

1. In 1773, ... crossed the Arctic Circle for the first time.
   - a. Captain James Cook
   - b. Joseph Cook
   - c. James Swift
   - d. James Cooper
2. .... is the southern-most active volcano in the world.
   - a. Mt. Fujiyama
   - b. Mt. Vesuvius
   - c. Mt. Erebus
   - d. Mt. Etna
3. The winter season in Antarctica lasts ....
   - a. from October to December
   - b. from March to September
   - c. throughout the year
   - d. None of the above
4. The Antarctic Treaty was signed in the year ....
   - a. 1969
   - b. 1959
   - c. 1988
   - d. 1999

C. Answer these questions in brief.

1. Explain the location of Antarctica.
2. What is an ice shelf?
3. Name the mountain range located in East Antarctica.
4. Write the names of the research stations set up by India in Antarctica.

D. Answer these questions in detail.

1. Explain the main physical divisions of Antarctica.
2. Explain the location of the Southern or the Antarctic Ocean.
3. Write a short note on the flora and fauna of Antarctica.
4. Write a short note on the climate of Antarctica.
5. Why was the Antarctic Treaty signed?

E. Map Work

On an outline map of Antarctica, mark the following:

1. Mt. Erebus
2. Southern Sea
3. South Pole

4. Ross Sea
5. Dakshin Gangotri Research Centre
6. Lesser Antarctica

Think Box

Unlike the Arctic, where a large area of sea ice lasts throughout the year, the sea ice around Antarctica is thinner and nearly all of it melts during summer. Why do you think this happens?

Picture Study

Look at the picture and answer the questions.

1. Identify this bird.
2. Is this bird found in Antarctica?
3. Where else in the world is this bird found?

Life Skills and Values

Prepare a climate change awareness campaign plan. Include points such as impacts on ice, penguins, marine life and sea level. Suggest ways in which climate change can be controlled. Find out the names of two international organizations that work towards reducing the effects of climate change.

Enjoy

Imagine you are a scientist and have been sent to Bharti Research centre in Antarctica to study the climate problem. Answer the following questions based on your trip there:

1. What are the various climatic problems that we are facing right now?
2. What is the cause of climate change?

DIY

Look at the graph and answer the questions.

The graph shows the extent of the Antarctic sea ice during the months of February and September of each year from 1979 to September 2015 and February 2016. The minimum and maximum extent of the sea ice typically occurs in February and September each year.

February and September Monthly Average Antarctic Sea Ice Extent, 1979-2016

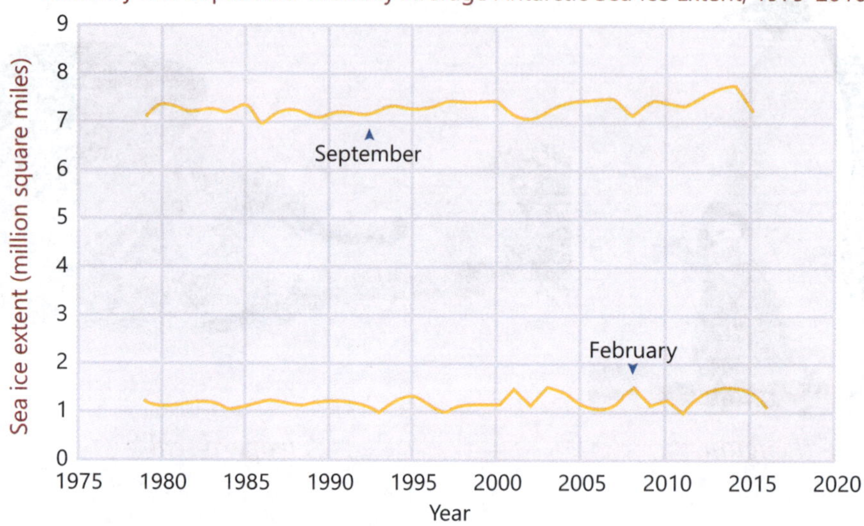

Data source: NSIDC (National Snow and Ice Data Center). 2016. Sea ice data and image archive.

1. In which year is the sea ice extent in September the largest?
2. In which year is the sea ice extent in February the largest?
3. What does this graph tell you about the overall sea ice of the Earth?

Geo Connect

Greenland is an island located in the Arctic Ocean. The ocean around Greenland is always frozen and the temperature of this region never rises beyond 10 degrees celsius. This region has amazing flora and fauna. The Arctic tern, Arctic willow, snow goose and the bowhead whale are some examples. The Inuit are the indigenous people of Greenland. They refer to themselves as Greenlanders. They have adapted to the cold and icy environment of this region.

In a Nutshell

- Antarctica is a continent located within the Antarctic Circle around the South Pole.
- Antarctica is divided into Greater and Lesser Antarctica.
- Antarctica is a cold desert, devoid of any plant or animal life.
- Antarctica has many scientific research stations from all around the world.

3. What will happen if no steps are taken to reduce the climate problem?
4. How has the climate problem affected Antarctica?
5. What were the methods you undertook in your research during your trip?
6. How can the people help in solving the climate problem?
7. Construct a line graph showing the rise in temperature in the last ten years.

Compile your data under the guidance of your language teacher into a 'research paper' and share your data with your classmates.

Weblinks

For more information, visit
http://polardiscovery.whoi.edu/antarctica/geography.html
Last accessed on 31/July/2020

11 Africa

Let's learn about...

- the location of Africa.
- the political divisions of Africa.
- the major physical features of Africa.

Key Terms

- Africa
- Suez Canal
- Sahara
- Horn of Africa

Reflect

I am known as the most mysterious land, especially among the Europeans, as they were unable to explore the interior part of my landmass. Thus, they named me the 'Dark Continent'. Can you guess my name?

Location and Size

Africa is the second largest continent in the world. It is three times the size of Europe. Africa covers about one-fifth of the Earth's total surface. The continent is bound by the Atlantic Ocean in the west, the Mediterranean Sea in the north and the Red Sea and the Indian Ocean in the east. The Mediterranean Sea separates Africa from Europe and the Red Sea separates it from Asia. The Isthmus of Suez connects Africa to Asia.

AFRICA AT A GLANCE

Latitudinal extent: 37°N to 35°S
Longitudinal extent: 51°E to 16°W
Highest point: Mt.Kilimanjaro
Lowest point: Lake Assal
No. of countries: 54
Population density: 45 per sq km

The equator passes through Africa and divides it almost into two equal halves. The Tropic of Cancer and the Tropic of Capricorn pass through the north and the south of Africa respectively. The Prime Meridian passes through Africa near the east of Accra in Ghana.

Suez Canal

Political Divisions

Africa is divided into five major political divisions—northern, eastern, central, western and southern Africa.

Northern Africa

Northern Africa extends from Morocco in the east to Sudan in the west. It is bordered on three sides by the north Atlantic Ocean, the Mediterranean Sea and the Red Sea. The countries located in Northern Africa are Morocco, Algeria, Tunisia, Libya, Egypt and Sudan.

Eastern Africa

The countries of Eastern Africa are Djibouti, Eritrea, Ethiopia, Kenya, Somalia, Tanzania and Uganda. This region extends from the Red Sea to Mozambique. It includes the Horn of Africa and the island of Madagascar.

Central Africa

The countries located in Central Africa are Burundi, Cameroon, Central African Republic, Chad, the Republic of Congo, the Democratic Republic of Congo, Gabon, Rwanda, São Tomé and Príncipe and parts of Guinea.

Western Africa

The countries located in Western Africa are Benin, Burkina Faso, Cape Verde, Gambia, Ghana, Guinea, Guinea-Bissau, Ivory Coast, Liberia, Mali, Mauritania, Niger, Nigeria, Senegal, Sierra Leone and Togo. Most of the West African countries are located along the Atlantic coastline. Mali, Burkina Faso and Niger have no direct access to the sea. The West African countries are located on the trading crossroads, connecting Africa, Europe and North and South America.

FactPedia

Addis Ababa is the capital and the chief commercial capital of Ethiopia. Nairobi is the capital of Kenya and the main commercial center of Kenya.

Southern Africa

The countries of Southern Africa are Angola, Botswana, Lesotho, Malawi, Mozambique, Namibia, South Africa, Swaziland, Zambia and Zimbabwe.

Physical Divisions

Africa has eight major physical divisions:

- Sahara
- Ethiopian Highlands
- Swahili Coast
- Great African Lakes
- Sahel
- Savanna
- Rainforest
- Southern Africa

Figure Out

Find out from your history teacher about how India had close relations with South Africa.

Horn of Africa: the easternmost peninsular region of Africa, comprising Djibouti, Eritrea, Ethiopia and Somalia

Africa, Political

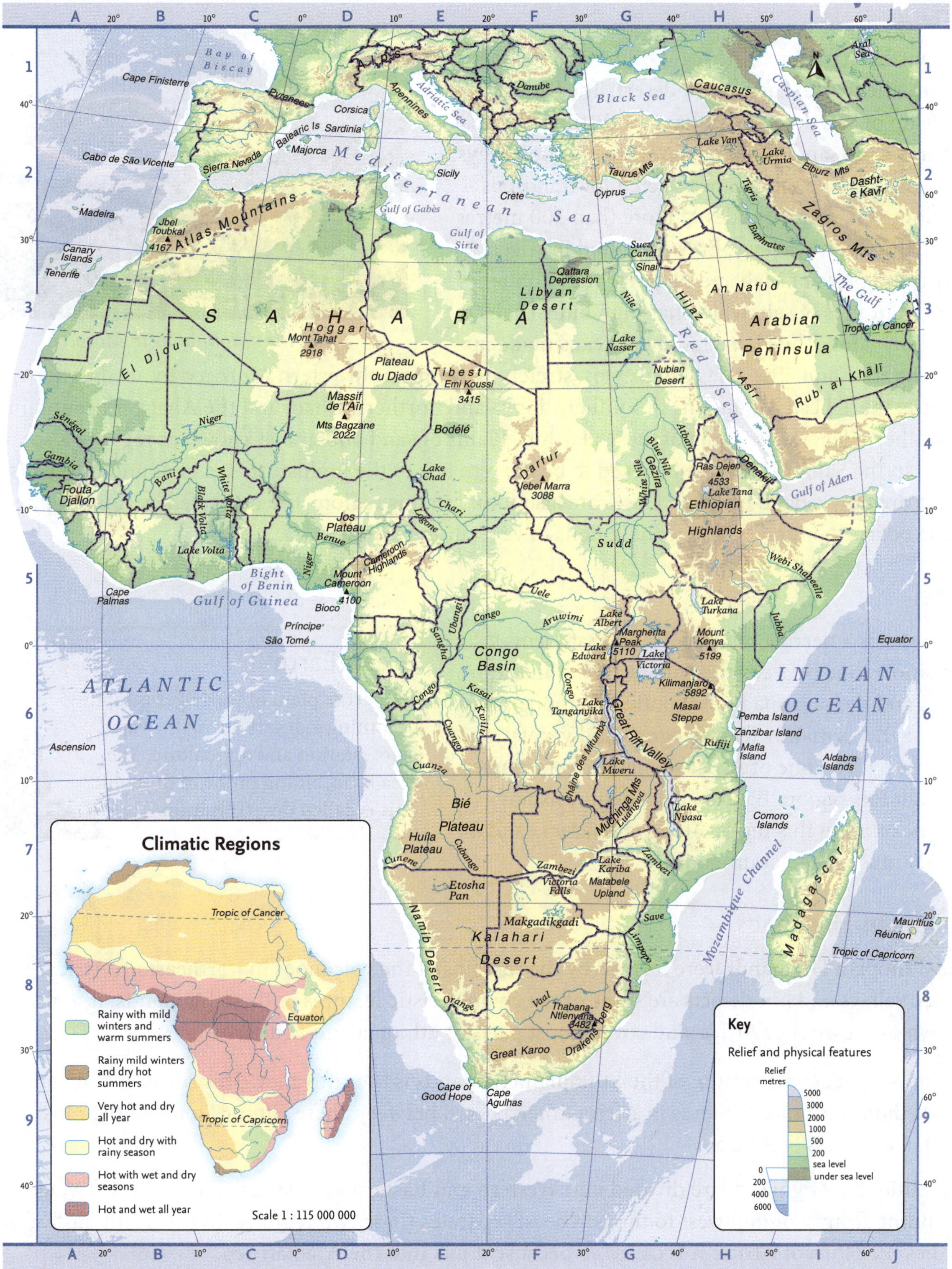

Africa, Physical

Sahara

The Atlas Mountains in Morocco

The northern region of Africa is dominated by the Sahara, the world's largest hot desert. The Sahara is made up of a rocky plain. It has two distinct physical features—the sand dunes or the ergs, and the valleys or the wadis. The sand dunes stretch for hundreds of kilometers with altitudes of more than 300 metres above the mean sea level. Ergs are found in Algeria, Libya, and parts of Mali and Nigeria. They contain large quantities of salt, which has high industrial and food value. The Hamadas are plateaus made up of rocks and sand. The Atlas Mountains, stretching from southwestern Morocco to northeastern Tunisia, the Tibesti Mountains in southern Libya and northern Chad, and the Ahaggar Mountains in southern Algeria are some of these plateaus. Plains of sand and gravel known as regs are also found in the Sahara. They are believed to be the remains of the prehistoric sea beds and riverbeds which are now devoid of water. Oases are also found in this region. The oases, fed by rain, trapped in the bedrock or gravel, also form regions of vegetation in the Sahara.

Sahel

The Sahel is a narrow semi-arid land that forms a transition zone between the Sahara Desert in the north and the savanna in the south. The topography of the Sahel is mainly flat with grassland vegetation. The river Niger, one of Africa's longest rivers, passes through this region. Baobab, a drought resistant tree, is found in this region along with acacia and a prickly grass called cram-cram.

Green Earth

The fertile plain of the Niger is rapidly becoming a desert due to the rapid deforestation and agriculture. The area is becoming prone to drought. This is called desertification.

Ethiopian Highlands

The Ethiopian Highlands were formed by the remains of the volcanoes in northeastern Africa. Tall peaks, valleys and hot deserts are some of the characteristic features of these highlands. It is also known as the 'roof of Africa' and covers most parts of Ethiopia and Eritrea.

The most spectacular feature of the Ethiopian Highlands is the rift valley. This rift system extends across thousands of kilomteres in Africa. Interspersed between these rifts are some of the most spectacular lakes of Africa.

The Ethiopian Highlands are divided into Western and Eastern Highlands. The Great Rift Valley extending from the southwest to the northeast separates these two regions. To the north-east of the rift lies the Horn of Africa. It is called so because it juts into the Arabian Sea.

interspersed: scattered between or among other things

Savanna

Serengeti Plains, Tanzania

The savanna is a region of tropical grasslands which covers most of the central African region. It stretches from the south of Sahel to the north of southern Africa. The savanna of Africa experiences a wet and dry tropical climate. The topography is dominated by rolling grasslands with dotted trees. The Serengeti Plains are the most well-known regions of the African savanna. It is a vast plain that extends from Massai-Mara in Kenya to the Serengeti National Park in Tanzania.

Swahili Coast

The Swahili Coast is the southeastern coast of Africa along the Indian Ocean. It mainly comprises Kenya, Tanzania and Mozambique. The islands lying off the Swahili Coast—Zanzibar, Pate and Comoros—in the Indian Ocean, also belong to this region. The nearby coral reefs and the barrier islands protect the coast from severe weather. This region is inhabited by the Swahili people. It is an economically significant region as it acts as a gateway of trade between Africa and Asia.

Rainforests

African rainforests

The African rainforests spread across East, Central and West Africa. Almost one-third of these forests are located in central Africa. Most of these rainforests are concentrated in Cameroon, Congo, Democratic Republic of Congo, Gabon, Ghana, Ivory Coast, Liberia and Nigeria. However, the African rainforests are shrinking at an alarming rate. Presently, most of Africa's rainforests are found in the Congo river basin on the Atlantic Ocean side of the continent.

African Great Lakes

The African Great Lakes or the East African Lakes are a group of lakes in eastern Africa. These lakes were formed by massive fissures on the Earth's surface. Most of these rivers are located in the East African Rift System spanning across nine countries. The African Great Lakes are listed below.

- Lake Malawi is located in the southern region of the Rift Valley. It drains into the Zambezi River.
- Lakes Tanganyika and Kivu are located in the Congo river basin.
- Lakes Edward and Albert of the Nile river drainage system flow along the western branch of the Rift Valley.
- Lake Victoria is located in a shallow depression formed between the eastern and the western rift highlands. It is the second-largest freshwater lake in the world. It is divided among Uganda, Tanzania and Kenya.

- Lake Victoria is the source of the river Nile.
- Lake Malawi is located between Malawi, Mozambique and Tanzania. It is the third-largest and second-deepest lake in Africa. The largest river flowing into it is the Ruhuhu River.
- The Lake Malawi National Park is located at the southern end of the great expanse of Lake Malawi.
- Lake Rudolf is located in northern Kenya. The lake has brackish waters because of the absence of an outlet. Three rivers namely the Omo, Turkwel and Kerio flow into Lake Rudolf.

Lake Victoria in Uganda

Lake Malawi

The other lakes include:

Lake	Location	Features
Lake Albert	Uganda and Congo	Largest oil producing shore in sub-Saharan Africa
Lake Edward	Uganda and Congo	Smallest of the lakes; home to many perennial and migratory bird species
Lake Kivu	Congo and Rwanda	Volcanic eruptions have separated Lake Kivu from Lake Edward; largest island–Idjwi
Lake Tanganyika	Congo and Tanzania	Longest freshwater lake in the world; second-deepest lake in the world; Kalambo Falls, the second-highest uninterrupted waterfall in Africa is located near the southern shore of Lake Tanganyika

The African Great Lakes region has a diverse range of aquatic and terrestrial animal life. This region is the homeland of hippopotamuses and crocodiles. This region has also migrating savanna animals such as wildebeest. They use the lakes as watering holes that is a source of drinking water.

brackish: salty; sub-Saharan Africa: the part of the African continent that lies to the south of the Sahara Desert

Southern Africa

Southern Africa is located in the southernmost region of Africa. The topography is dominated by an undulating plateau that descends in mighty shelves toward the south-eastern lowlands. The Drakensberg Mountains separate the plateau from the lowland regions. The southern point of Africa is known as Cape Agulhas. The beginning of the line of demarcation between the Atlantic and the Indian oceans starts here. The Cape of Agulhas is spectacular as it consists of a gradually curving coastline.

Drakensberg Mountains

The Kalahari Desert forms the central depression of the Southern African plateau. The southern part of this plateau ends in the Great Escarpment. The Kalahari has more flora and fauna than a true desert. It is a huge stretch of red sand without any surface water. The only permanent river is the Okavango. The southern Zimbabwe and much of South Africa are regions of grasslands and scrublands known as the veld. The Namib Desert lies on the coastal regions of Namibia. It is uninhabited by people except for a few indigenous pastoral groups.

Drainage

- The Nile is the longest river in the world. It has its source in Lake Victoria. The Mediterranean Sea is the mouth of the Nile. The river is navigable and is also known as the 'lifeline of Egypt'.
- The Congo River is the second-longest river in Africa. It is the deepest river in the world. The source of the Congo River is in the mountains and highlands of the East African Rift System, and the Lakes Tanganyika and Mweru.

The Nile, Aswan, Egypt

- The Niger is the third-longest river in Africa. Its main tributary is the Benue River. The river floods almost every year. The Niger has a very unique course as it moves away from the sea into the Sahara Desert and takes a right turn near the ancient city of Timbuktu.
- The Zambezi is the fourth longest river in Africa. It is the largest river that flows into the Indian Ocean. The river flows through Angola, Botswana, Malawi, Mozambique, Namibia, Tanzania, Zambia and Zimbabwe. The Victoria Falls are located on the Zambezi River.

Victoria Falls

The African continent has huge geographical diversity ranging from the hottest desert to the longest river. Africa is the second largest continent with a huge reserve of natural bounty. The NASA satellite images of Africa is used to study the agricultural pattern, geology, forestry and meteorology. If you look at the satellite images of Africa, you will find that Africa has a huge geographical diversity with the desert area in the north, the fertile plains in the center and varied topography in the south.

DIY

Complete this Africa quiz.

1. Name seven African countries whose names start with the letter M.
2. Which country is located on the southernmost point of Africa?
3. Addis Ababa is the capital city of which African country?
4. Which lake is located largely in Tanzania and Uganda and is bordered by Kenya?
5. Which country is located between Sierra Leone and Cote D'Ivore?

Geo Connect

The Black Rock desert is located in northwestern Nevada in the United States. This desert region has many landforms that were formed by volcanic activity. This region is marked by hot springs, scattered over a large area. Another spectacular feature of this region is the Playa. A Playa is a flat depression found in the desert region which is periodically filled with water. The Quinn River is the largest river of this region. It is an intermittent stream.

In a Nutshell

- Africa is the second-largest continent in the world. It is bound by the Atlantic Ocean in the west, by the Mediterranean Sea in the north and the Red Sea and the Indian Ocean in the east.
- The political divisions of Africa are the Northern Africa, Eastern Africa, Central Africa, Western Africa and Southern Africa.
- The eight physical divisions of Africa are the Sahara Desert, the Sahel, Ethiopian Highlands, the savanna, the Swahili coast, the rainforest, the African Great Lakes and Southern Africa.
- The Nile, the Congo, the Niger and the Zambezi are the major rivers of Africa.

Workout

A. Fill in the blanks.

1. The African continent is bound by the .... in the west, ... in the north, and .... in the east. The .... Sea separates Africa from Europe and the .... Sea from Asia.
2. .... is a narrow band of semi-arid land between Sahara and the savanna.
3. The .... is the longest river in the world.
4. Three rivers namely the Omo, Turkwel and Kerio flow into Lake ....

B. Choose the correct answer and fill in the blanks.

1. Africa is the .... largest continent.
   a. third b. second c. fourth d. fifth
2. The .... River flows through Africa.
   a. Nile b. Thames c. Ganga d. Rhone
3. Ergs are not found in ....
   a. Algeria b. Libya c. Mali d. Somalia
4. .... is the part of the African continent that lies to the south of the Sahara Desert.
   a. Northern Africa b. Western Africa
   c. Southern Africa d. Sub-Saharan Africa
5. .... is the second deepest lake in Africa.
   a. Lake Turkana b. Lake Malawi c. Lake Victoria d. Lake Edward

C. Complete the following tables.

Political division of Africa	Countries (any 2)
Eastern Africa	
	Morocco and Sudan
Central Africa	
Southern Africa	
	Mali and Ivory Coast

D. Give one word for the following:

1. It connects Africa to Asia: ....
2. Source of the river Nile: ....
3. Regions of grasslands and scrublands in Africa: ....
4. Longest river in the world: ....
5. Longest freshwater lake in the world: ....

E. Give reasons for the following.

1. The Horn of Africa is called so.
2. The Niger is becoming prone to drought.
3. Lake Rudolf has brackish waters.
4. The Nile has been called the lifeline of Africa.

F. Answer these questions in brief.

1. What is the 'Horn of Africa'?
2. What are wildebeest? Where are they found?
3. Define:

   a. Ergs b. Cram-cram c. Wadis d. Oasis
4. Name any five great lakes of Africa.

G. Answer these questions in detail.

1. Write a short note on:

   a. The Sahara Desert b. The Savannah

   c. Ethiopian Highlands d. Kalahari Desert
2. Write a short note on the Great African Lakes.
3. Describe the East African Rift System.
4. Explain the relief features of the Sahara and the Sahel.

H. Map Work

On the map of Africa mark the following:

- River Malawi
- Kalahari Desert
- Victoria Lake
- River Nile
- River Congo
- Sahara Desert

Think Box

How did the formation of the rift valleys in Africa affect the formation of the continents?

Picture Study

Look at the picture and answer the questions.

1. This the longest river in the world. Identify it.
2. Name the source and the mouth of the river.
3. Name the countries it flows through.

Life Skills and Values

Nobel Prize Winner, Nelson Mandela led South Africa's transition from white-minority rule in the 1990s after being in prison for 27 years because of his political activities. On 5 December, 2013 he died. Nelson Mandela played an important role in ending apartheid in Africa.

Conduct a group discussion in your class addressing the following topics:

1. Who was Nelson Mandela? What role did he play in the politics of Africa?
2. How did the world react to the death of this personality?
3. How does he inspire you?

Enjoy

Be a travel guide

Imagine you are a travel guide in Africa and a foreign group is scheduled to come. Make a small travel book for the tourists so that they can understand Africa better. Make sure you include the following points:

1. Brief history of the African continent
2. Geographical and topographical changes in the continent of Africa over the ages
3. What are the various places to see in Africa and how do you plan to take them to those places?
4. Why is Africa a unique continent?

With the help of your history teacher, explore the history of Africa with a special reference to the ancient Nile valley civilization. With the help of your geography teacher, find out about the topographical changes in Africa. Also, find out about the impact of urbanization on the 'Dark Continent.' With the help of your English teacher, compile the information and present the data in an innovative way.

Weblinks

For more information, visit
https://www.nationsonline.org/oneworld/africa.htm
Last accessed on 31/July/2020

12 Cocoa Cultivation in Ghana

Let's learn about...

- the location of Ghana
- the physical features of Ghana
- the cultivation and processing of cocoa in Ghana

Key Terms

- cocoa
- plantations
- chocolate

Reflect

Cocoa is a valuable crop that is sometimes referred to as 'food of the gods'. Our .... originates from cocoa beans, which come from cocoa pods that grow on cocoa trees.

Ghana is a country located along the Gulf of Guinea and the Atlantic Ocean in Western Africa. The country is bordered by the Ivory Coast in the west, Burkina Faso in the north, Togo in the east and the Gulf of Guinea and the Atlantic Ocean in the south. It is located only a few degrees away from the equator. Thus, the climate here is hot and humid. The prime meridian passes through Ghana through the port town of Tema. Ghana is a leading country in the production of cocoa. To study the reasons behind Ghana becoming the leading producer of cocoa cultivation, let us take a quick overview of the physical features of Ghana.

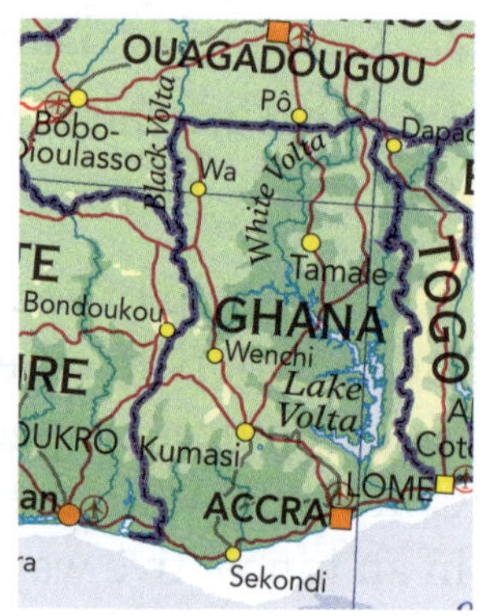

Ghana

Physical Features

Ghana is divided into five different geographical units. They are the Coastal Plain, the Akwapim-Togo Ranges, the Ashanti Uplands, the Volta Basin and the High Plains.

The Coastal Plain

The low coastal plain stretches across the southern part of Ghana. It has four sub-regions namely, the coastal savanna, the Volta delta, the Accra plains and the Akan lowlands. The coastal plain is intersected by several rivers and streams which are navigable by canoe. The region is dotted with sandy palm-fringed beach. Small-scale farming and fishing are carried out in this region.

The Akwapim-Togo Ranges

The Akwapim-Togo Ranges are narrow belts of ridges and hills in eastern Ghana. They extend from the Densu river on the Atlantic coast to the boundary with Togo. The hills continue eastward to the Niger River as the Togo Mountains in Togo and the Atakora Mountains in Benin. The Volta river flows through these ranges. The catchment area of the Volta River region is important for cash crops of cacao and coffee. This region has semi-deciduous forest cover. The slopes are steep and marked by abrupt cliffs.

The Ashanti Uplands

The Ashanti Uplands lie to the north of the Akan lowlands. They stretch from the Ivory Coast border in the west to the elevated edge of the Volta Basin in the east. The Kwahu Plateau has an average elevation of about 450 meters above the sea level. This area produces most of the country's cocoa and the tropical forest continues to be a vital source of timber for the lumber industry of Ghana.

FactPedia

Kumasi is Ghana's second-largest city located in the Ashanti Uplands. Obuasi and Konongo, two important gold mining centres, are also located here.

The Volta Basin

The Volta is an important river of Ghana. It occupies the central part of the country and covers about 45 per cent of the total area of Ghana. The basin is made up of volcanic sandstone and has infertile soil.

River Volta, Ghana

High Plains

The high plains are located in the northern and the northwestern part of Ghana. The soils of the high plains are more arable than those of the Volta basin.

Climate

Ghana lies in the torrid zone. Thus, it has a warm and humid climate. The temperature in the extreme north is higher as compared to the coastal regions. The southwestern part of Ghana experiences a hot and humid climate whereas the northern part of the country experiences a hot and dry climate. Ghana has two main seasons—the wet and the dry season. Rainfall is more in the southwestern part of the country.

Cocoa Cultivation in Ghana

Cocoa cultivation is the most important economic activity in Ghana as it accounts for more than 60 per cent of its export. The cultivation of cocoa started in the coastal district of Ghana but over time, it spread about 700 kilometers inland. The greatest concentration of cocoa cultivation is in the cocoa triangle comprising the towns of Accra, Kumasi and Takoradi. Cocoa cultivation in Ghana gained impetus because of improved agricultural practices, better quality stock and the use of fertilizers.

FactPedia
The northeastern part of Ghana experiences Harmattan, a dry desert wind that blows in the month of December to March, origanating from the Sahara Desert. These winds cause hot days and cool nights in the northern part of Ghana.

The cocoa plantations in Ghana are small farms most of which do not exceed a hectare.

Although cocoa is an important crop of Ghana, farmers also grow oil palms, coffee, rice, coconuts yams and cassava.

Growing conditions

Cocoa is a fairly adaptable crop and can grow under varied conditions. It has three main requirements. They are reasonably fertile soil, a warm and moist climate, and forest protection.

- The equatorial environment of Ghana facilitates the cultivation of cocoa. Cocoa needs high temperatures and well-distributed heavy rainfall. A cocoa plant can tolerate a short dry season with annual rainfall of around 1270 mm to 2030 mm. It is sensitive to prolonged droughts and cannot grow in regions with low humidity. Thus, the climate of Ghana is suitable for cocoa cultivation.

A cocoa plantation

- Cocoa is also sensitive to direct sunlight. The ample forest cover in Ghana helps the crop grow. Ghana farmers maintain the forest cover by retaining the remnant forest cover. They grow coco-yam, papaya and banana which provide commercial returns.
- The well-drained and deep soil with rich humus content facilitates the growth of cocoa in Ghana.
- Cocoa cultivation is labour intensive. More human labour is required right from plantation to harvest of the cocoa fruits.

Figure Out
The cocoa cultivation in Ghana was 969 tonnes in 2016-17 but dropped to 850 tonnes in 2019-2020. What were the reasons for the drop in cocoa cultivation in Ghana?

Cultivation

A cocoa plant

The cocoa plant is cultivated in small farms most of which are not more than a hectare in size. The bush is cleared in the dry season and the new seeds are planted. The new seeds are transplanted at a distance when the seedlings become 4.5 cm tall. Unlike the wild cocoa tree, the cultivated trees are pruned to a height of 6 and 7 meters and are usually replaced after 20 to 30 years. The trees start flowering when the plant is 4 to 5 years old. The flowers are small and yellow and they develop into pods which ripen in about 5-6 months. The number of pods that a cocoa tree bears depends on the variety and the age of the tree. The cocoa plants start with a limited number of pods and each year the numbers keep increasing until it reaches its peak of productivity at the age of ten or twelve. The pods are about 15 to 20 cm long.

Harvesting

Cocoa farming in Ghana

Ghana enjoys two harvest seasons. The main harvest season is from the month of October to January. These months experience the dry season in West Africa. The second harvest season lasts from March to May. The farmers begin harvesting early in the morning. The pod has to be picked carefully as they are very delicate. Pod-pickers called tumbadour separate the ripe melon-shaped pods without bruising the bark. The picker uses a large handle hooked knife for the high pods. They avoid climbing the trees. The pods are sliced off with a cutlass known as a machete. They are cut open and the pulp inside is extracted. Each pod contains about 30 to 40 small seeds.

DIY

Complete this chocolate quiz.

1. When and where was the first chocolate bar made?
2. Which countries are the top two producers of cocoa in the world?
3. Which essential minerals are found in chocolate?
4. Why is cocoa called the 'food of gods'?
5. Which companies are the two biggest chocolate producers in the world?
6. What is the percentage share of the price of a chocolate bar that the cocoa farmers receive?
7. What does the Fairtrade mark indicate on a chocolate bar?
8. What is the 'Make Chocolate Fair!' Campaign? What are its objectives?

cutlass: a short sword with a curved blade

Fermentation

The distinct chocolate flavour of the cocoa beans is because of fermentation. Unfermented cocoa beans are not used to make chocolates. The beans that are still covered with pulp are heaped on the ground or into a basket and covered with large banana leaves to be left for the three to eight days. The beans are not washed until they are fermented. When the beans have fermented, they have a rich brown colour. They are thoroughly dried up in the sun or indoors with hot air blowers. Cocoa beans are vulnerable to infestation and mold. Therefore, they are stored in sacks.

Selling

The farmers sell their produce in the market. Farmers staying in small isolated villages usually get the product to the market by transporting it there by themselves. The buyers prefer to buy the properly ripe and fermented cocoa seeds. Purple or slate colour seeds are usually rejected. The busiest shipping season is from November to April.

FactPedia

Takoradi is an artificial harbour built to facilitate the export of cocoa, in December 1928. The main importing ports are London, Le Havre, Hamburg, Marseilles, New York and Orleans.

Processing

The cocoa seeds are taken to the factory where they are sorted, cleaned and further roasted to a dark brown colour. The cocoa nib of the beans is crushed and ground to produce the chocolate liquor which is used as a base for making chocolate and other cocoa products.

Future of Cocoa Industry in Ghana

The cocoa industry plays a major role in the economy of Ghana. It provides employment to the people and dominates the export market of the country.

Government policy plays an important role in the development of this industry. The government has taken steps to develop good agricultural practices like use of good fertilizers and pesticides to intensify cocoa production.

Europe and North America are two of the leading buyers of cocoa. Cadbury and Nestle are the leading manufacturers of chocolate and chocolate by-products like cocoa butter.

Geo Connect

Just like cocoa plantation in Ghana, the islands of the Caribbean region are famous for sugarcane plantations. Though both sugarcane and cocoa are tropical crops, there are differences between their methods of cultivation. Sugarcane processing units are located near to the farm because this perishable plant has to be processed within a few hours from harvesting.

infestation: a large number of insects that often destroy stored items

In a Nutshell

- Ghana lies in the tropical region. The geographical and climatic factors allow Ghana to be the leading producer of cocoa.
- Cocoa has three main requirements namely, reasonably fertile soil, a warm moist climate, and forest protection.
- The cocoa plant is cultivated in small farms most of which are not more than a hectare in size.
- Ghana enjoys two harvest seasons—from October to January and from March to May.
- The distinct chocolate flavour of the cocoa beans is because of fermentation.
- Exporting cocoa is a major economic activity of Ghana.
- European and American countries are major buyers of cocoa from Ghana.

Workout

A. Fill in the blanks.

1. Ghana is located along the .... and the .... Ocean in Western Africa.
2. ...., ... and .... form the cocoa triangle.
3. .... and .... are the leading manufacturers of chocolate.
4. The .... of the beans is crushed and ground to produce the chocolate liquor which is used as a base for making chocolate and other cocoa products.

B. Fill in the blanks with the correct answers.

1. Cocoa is a .... plant.
   a. tropical   b. temperate   c. frigid   d. tundra
2. Ghana enjoys .... harvest seasons.
   a. one   b. two   c. three   d. four
3. .... is a by-product of the cocoa cultivation.
   a. cocoa butter   b. cocoa jelly   c. chocolate   d. caramel

C. Give reasons.

1. The busiest shipping season of cocoa in Ghana is from November to April.
2. Cocoa cultivation in Ghana dropped in 1977.
3. Cocoa grows well in Ghana.

D. Answer these questions in brief.

1. Into how many geographical units is Ghana divided? Name them.
2. Explain the location of:
   a. The Ashanti Uplands   b. The Volta Basin
   c. The Akwapim-Togo ranges   d. High plains

3. Name three other crops grown by people of Ghana other than cocoa.
4. What kind of soil favours cocoa cultivation?
5. How do buyers choose the good cocoa beans?

E. Answer these questions in detail.

1. Based on the climate of Ghana, answer the following:
   a. What type of climate does Ghana experience?
   b. How many seasons does Ghana experience? Name them.
   c. What is the Harmattan? When does it blow?
2. Based on cocoa cultivation, answer the following:
   a. How many times is cocoa harvested in Ghana? What is the duration of each harvesting season?
   b. Who harvests them and how?
   c. How is cocoa fermented? What role does fermentation play in the development of chocolate?

F. Map Work

On a map of Ghana, locate the following:

- Ashanti Uplands
- The cocoa triangle
- Artificial habours at Takoradi
- Obuasi and Konongo

Think Box

Cocoa is cultivated in Ghana but the best chocolates are made in Switzerland. Find out the reasons for this.

Picture Study

Look at the picture and answer the questions.

1. Identify this crop.
2. What type of soil is necessary for the crop?
3. What is the harvest season of this crop?

Life Skills and Values

You have learnt that cocoa plantation affects the forest cover of Ghana even though it is an important source of income in the region. Have a group discussion regarding how to maintain a balance between environmental protection and the cultivation of cocoa.

Enjoy

Be a cocoa cultivator

You are a cocoa cultivator and you have recently bought land in Ghana which you want to employ in cocoa cultivation. Make a plan about how you would cultivate cocoa effectively on your land. Write a report talking about the following:

1. Soil
    a. What nutrients are present in the soil that will help cocoa to grow?
    b. Which nutrients are deficient in the soil of your land? How do you plan on overcoming this nutrient deficiency?
2. Protection of crops
    a. Cocoa is prone to pests. How would you remove pests from your land and ensure proper protection of your crops?
3. Land usage
    a. How many trees do you want to grow per hectare on you field? What will be the expected produce per hectare from those trees?
    b. Where in your land do you plan to conduct fermentation and other processes involved in cocoa cultivation?
4. Market
    a. How do you plan to send your products to the market?

Weblinks

For more information, visit
http://agritech.tnau.ac.in/horticulture/horti_plantation%20crops_cocoa.html
Last accessed on 31/July/2020

13 Australia

Let's learn about...

- the location of Australia.
- the political divisions of Australia.
- the physical features of Australia.

Key Terms

- Oceania
- Great Barrier Reef
- Australiasia
- aborigines

Reflect

Name three countries located in the Southern Hemisphere of the Earth.

....

Australia is the smallest among the seven continents of the world. It is located entirely in the Southern Hemisphere between the Pacific and the Indian oceans. It comprises Australia and Tasmania. Along with New Zealand, Australia forms a wider region known as Oceania or Australasia.

AT A GLANCE

Latitude: 10° 41'S to 43° 38'S
Longitude: 113° 09'E to 153° 38'E
Longest mountain range: The Great Diving Range
Highest point: Mt. Kosciusko (2,226 m)
The lowest point: Lake Eyre
Largest Desert: Great Victoria Desert
Population density: 3 per sq. km

Australia is mainly located on the Indo-Australian Plate. The Australian landmass belongs to the ancient supercontinent Gondwana. Australia is a unique continent for many reasons.

- It is the only continent that does not have any active volcano.
- It is the driest inhabited continent.
- A major part of the continent is arid or semi-arid.
- Australia is one of the oldest landmasses where human inhabitation started more than 45,000 years ago. The native people of this continent are known as the aborigines.
- Australia is the only landmass on Earth which is a country as well as a continent.

Political Divisions

The Commonwealth of Australia comprises six states namely, New South Wales, Victoria, Queensland, South Australia, Western Australia and Tasmania. The capital of Australia is Canberra.

FactPedia

Australia was named in the 1970s. Meganesia was a name proposed in 1984 which meant the greater island or island group.

Oceania, Political

New South Wales

New South Wales lies in the southeastern part and is bound by the Pacific Ocean to the east, the states of Victoria to the south, South Australia to the west and Queensland to the north. Lord Howe Island in the Pacific Ocean is also a part of New South Wales. Sydney, the most populous and largest city of Australia, is its capital.

Victoria

Victoria is separated from New South Wales in the north by the Murray River. The Tasman Sea, the Indian Ocean and the Bass Strait lie on the southern coastline of Victoria. Melbourne is the capital of Victoria. The state gained economic importance after the discovery of petroleum and natural gas.

Melbourne, Australia

Queensland

Queensland occupies nearly one-fourth of Australia's landmass. It is the second largest state of Australia. Brisbane is the capital of Queensland. The Great Barrier Reef extends 2000 km off the Queensland's Coral Sea coastline. Despite its huge area, Queensland is thinly populated and most of the people live on the coastal regions of this state.

South Australia

Located in south-central Australia, it is one of the driest states of Australia. The Great Australian Bight, a portion of the Indian Ocean, lies to the south of Australia. Adelaide is the capital city of South Australia. The Great Victorian Desert lies to the west of South Australia.

Northern Territory

The Northern Territory is located in the central and northern region of Australia. It is largely tropical in the north and semi-arid in the far south. The capital city is Darwin. The northern territory is home to 400 species of birds. The flock bronzewing, a large pigeon, is found in this region. The rugged central and northern regions are home to various birds like the singing bush lark and the buttonquail. The wetland region is home to wading shore birds and geese. The white-throated grasswren, the banded fruit dove and the chestnut-quilled rock pigeon are all endemic to the Northern Territory.

Pillar formation, the Great Victorian Desert

Western Australia

Western Australia, as the name suggests, occupies the western part of the continent. Western Australia is a place of contrasts with desert regions in the east and a long coastline in the west. The state's capital is Perth, the fourth-most populous city in Australia.

Perth skyline

A majority of the population lives in Perth and Greater Perth which is one of the largest metropolitan regions in Australia. Western Australia is home to a wild range of flora and fauna. The southwestern part is a hotspot of biodiversity. The economy of Western Australia is largely based on agriculture.

Tasmania

Tasmania is an island state of Australia. It is also known as Van Diemen's land. Tasmania is separated from the mainland by the Bass Strait. It is said to be an extension of the Great Dividing Range. The state comprises the main island, Tasmania, along with Bruny Island and the King and Flinders Islands. Tasmania is the smallest state of Australia. It is essentially a mountainous island and its highest peak is Mount Ossa.

Wineglass Bay, Freycinet National Park, Tasmania

Physical Features

Australia has four main physical divisions:

- Eastern Highlands
- Western Plateau
- Central Lowlands
- Coastal Plains

The Eastern Highlands

The Eastern Highlands of Australia extend from the tip of the Cape York Peninsula in the north to the Grampians in Victoria. They are also called the Great Divide or Great Dividing Range. They stretch for about 4000 km. The highland divides the surface run-off into the eastern and the western flowing rivers. Towards the east of the range, the rivers flow into the Pacific Ocean and to the west, the rivers end in the salt lakes. The erosion of the Great Divide has formed the Great Escarpment on their eastern, seaward side. Many places along this region are rugged and filled with numerous hills, valleys, cliffs and gorges. This region is fertile and is made of young rocks. This geographical region is the highest part of Australia. This region influences the climate of Australia by not allowing the rain-bearing winds to cross them leaving the Central Lowlands dry and the Coastal Plains rain-fed. Some major landforms of this region are Mount Kosciusko, Bass Strait and the Murray-Darling river basin.

Mount Feathertop, The Great Dividing Range

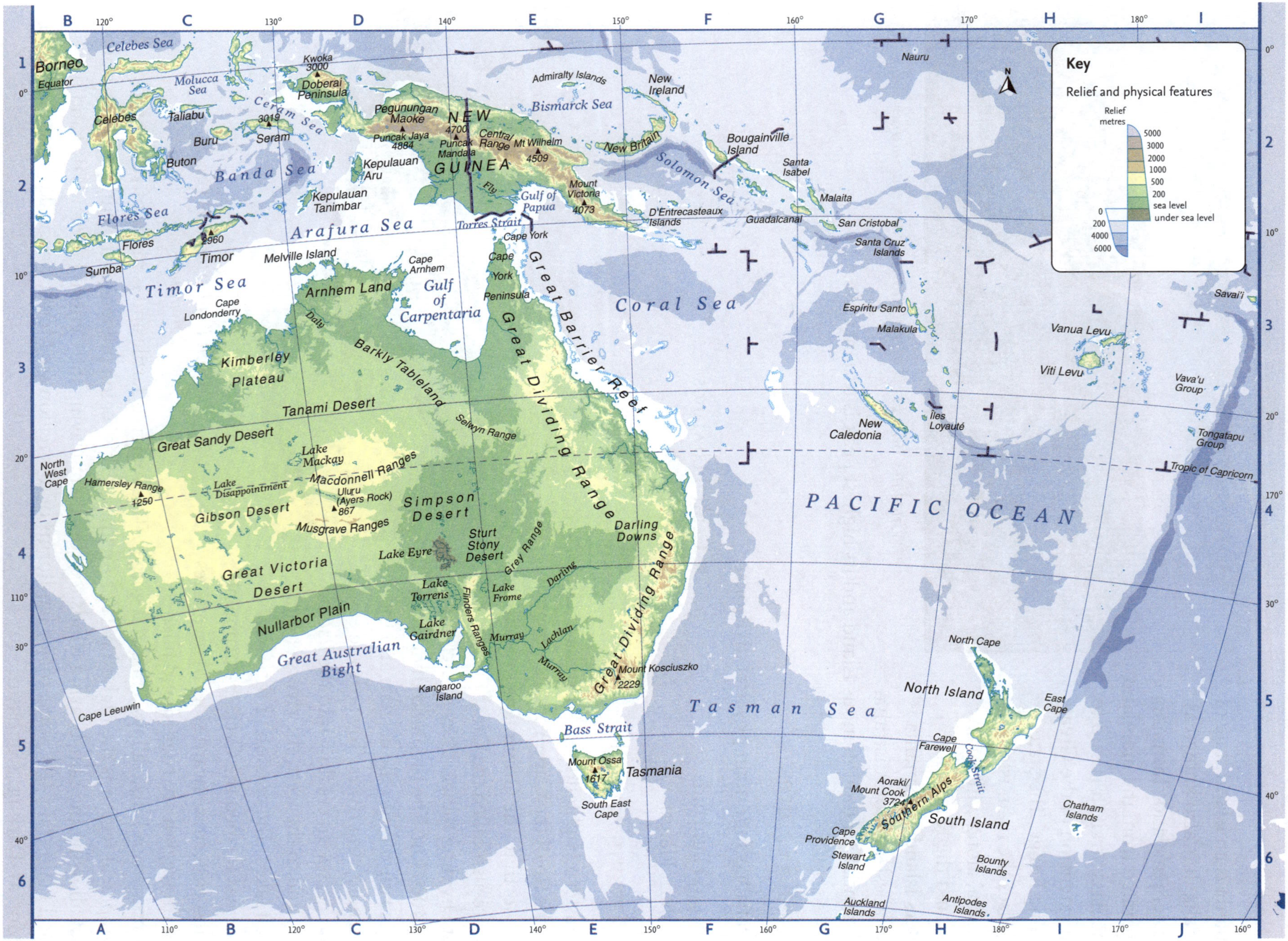

Oceania Physical

- The Murray and Darling rivers drain the largest landmass in Australia and together, they form the Murray-Darling river basin. This basin is home to many native flora and fauna. The Darling River has its source in northern New South Wales and meets the river Murray at Wentworth. The Murray River has its source in the Australian Alps. Lake Alexandrina and the Lake Coorong are some of the important lakes. The entire Murray-Darling river system drains all of New South Wales, west of the Great Diving Range, parts of Victoria and southern Queensland. This basin is Australia's most important agricultural region. The most valuable resource of the region is water.

Murray Bridge, River Murray

- The Bass Strait separates Victoria from the island of Tasmania. It is approximately 250 km wide and 500 km long, with an average depth of 60 m. There are about fifty islands in the Bass Strait. The Bass Strait region gained economic importance after the discovery of oil fields in the Gippsland Basin. Some of the important oil fields include the Halibut Oil Field and the Kingfish Oil Field.

The Central Lowlands

The Central Lowlands are located in between the Murray-Darling basin to the north of the Gulf of Carpentaria. It passes through the Great Artesian Basin, which is one of the largest artesian groundwater basins in the world. This region is made up of sedimentary rocks.

FactPedia

The Cobbler Sandhills near lake Blanche, is an area in Strzelecki Desert, where the dunes are replaced by knolls or hillocks with vegetation cover on the top.

The Central Lowlands are mostly flatlands with occasional higher grounds in the form of desert ranges such as MacDonnell Ranges and the Musgrave Ranges. The Sturt Stony Desert, the Strzelecki Desert and the Simpson Desert are located in this region. Lake Eyre is also located in the Central Lowlands. The Strzelecki Desert is located to the northeast of Lake Eyre.

- The Simpson Desert is characterized by dune fields consisting of sword-shaped isolated dunes. The sand of the dune fields in the Simpson Desert display vibrant colours ranging from white to dark red.

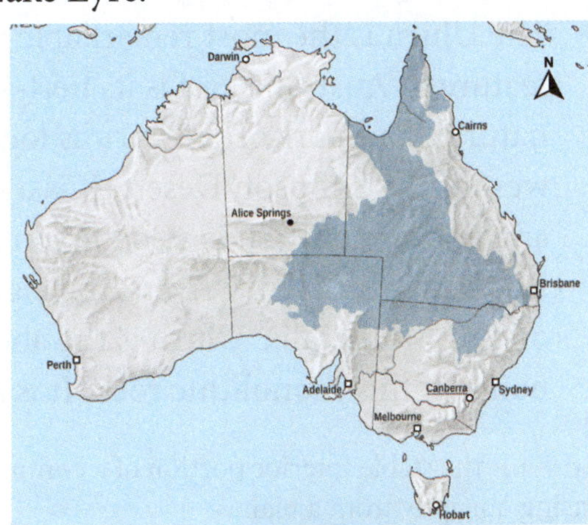

- The Great Artesian Basin is one of Australia's largest groundwater basins. It underlies an area of about 1.7 million square kilometres beneath the arid and the semiarid region. This basin is the largest and the deepest artesian basin in the world. The water from the basin emerges naturally through the cracks in the rocks enclosing the water into springs, shallow water tables or into creeks and rivers creating a permanent water source, even during dry spells.

- Lake Eyre is a great saltwater lake and is also known as Kati Thanda. It lies in the southwestern corner of the Great Artesian Basin. It is a closed inland basin which is drained by intermittent streams. The lake is fed by a vast internal drainage system, but the rate of evaporation is so high that it dries up before it reaches the lake. Lake Eyre is usually dry but occasionally, it floods. This lake is considered to be the lowest point of the Australia continent. It is the largest saltwater lake and is known for its unusual pink hue.

Lake Eyre

The Western Plateau

The Western Plateau includes much of Western Australia and parts of South Australia and the Northern Territory. This region is the oldest part of the continent. It is also known as the Australian Shield. The rocks have a long geological history and have been exposed to the forces of erosion for almost the entire history of the Earth. This region is made up of igneous and metamorphic rocks. Some of the plateaus in this region are Kimberley, Hamersley and Yilgarn. These plateaus are partly based on cratons such as the Yilgarn Craton and Pilbara Craton. The Tropic of Capricorn passes through the Pilbara region. This region receives less rainfall and most of the region is flat and sandy with sparse vegetation cover. There are no permeant water courses as the region receives insufficient rainfall. Low rainfall makes this region arid and semiarid. The Western Plateau is low-lying due to the erosional activity by agents of gradation. Some of the remarkable landforms of this region are the Uluru, the Olgas, the Great Sandy Desert and the Great Victorian Desert.

Mitchell Falls, Kimberley, Western Austrlia

- The Uluru is the most remarkable geographical feature of Australia and is its best-known natural landmark. The Uluru is located on the west of the Simpson Desert. It is a massive, ancient monolith. It is also known as the Ayers Rock after Sir Henry Ayers, the eighth Premier of South Australia. Uluru is the aboriginal name of this monolithic rock. It is an inselberg,

The Uluru-Kata Tjuta National Park is home to different species of birds, animals and exceptional plants. This region is a paradise for birds. Visitors enjoy the rare opportunity to watch kangaroos, emus, dingos and wallabies roaming wild on the red, sandy stretch.

cratons: the stable interior portion of a continent made of ancient crystalline rock; inselberg: an isolated hill or mountain rising abruptly from a plain which literally means the island mountain. The surface is made up of valleys, ridges and caves formed due to erosional activity. However, the summit is flat. The Uluru displays a striking orange-red hue because of the surface oxidation of the iron content. The Uluru is a UNESCO World Heritage Site and is a significant part of the indigenous culture of Australia.

The Uluru

- The Olgas are a group of large-domed rock formations located towards the southwest of the Alice Spring. The name 'Olgas' means many heads. Unlike the Uluru, it is not a single massive rock structure but made of twenty-eight dome-like structures. The highest point of the Olgas is Mount Olga, which is about 546 m above sea level. The Olgas are composed of a conglomerate, a sedimentary rock with boulders of granite and basalt. The rocks are bound together by muddy and sandy sediments. The Olgas were formed because of the prolonged erosion of mountains.
- The Great Sandy Desert is another spectacular feature of Australia. It is a region of active sand dunes. This desert is the second-largest desert in Australia. It is a hot and dry desert made of dunes and ergs. It is also known as the Canning Desert. It is a vast, arid expanse of salt marshes and sand hills. The sand dunes are aligned to the prevailing winds and are blown from the east to the west. The plants growing in this region are mainly grasses, low woodland and thorny shrubs. The paperbark tree is a spectacular tree of this region which has layers of bark that resemble paper. This tree is found in the wetland of the desert. It has medicinal value as its oil serves as both an antiseptic and as an insect repellent. Desert bloodwood is another spectacular tree of this region. It stores water in the roots which helps the plant to survive in the hot drought. The Great Sandy Desert has a wet and dry climate. The wet season begins around November and ends around May.

Paperbark tree

DIY

Watch the movie *The Rabbit Proof Fence* which features the State Barrier Fence of Western Australia, the longest fence built by the Australian Government across the Great Sandy Desert. Find out why the Australian Government had built such a long fence. Parts of this fence still stand there. Discuss with your history teacher about the discovery of Australia and the fate of the aborigines.

- The Great Victoria Desert is the largest desert of Australia stretching for around 4,24,400 sq km. There are many small deserts on the border of the Great Victoria Desert. This desert consists of many sand hills, grassland plains, areas with a closely packed surface of pebbles and saltwater lakes. This region has red sand dunes, stony plains and dry salt lakes. On its north is the Gibson, a small sandy desert. The Tirai Desert and the Sturt Stony Desert lies to the east while the Nullarbor Plain lies to the south. A majority of people living in the region are indigenous Australians from different groups including the Kogara. The Nullarbor Plain is a dry land and is believed to be a dried sea bed. This is the world's largest limestone region and Australia's largest karst region. There are no trees in the Nullarbor region. There are, however, several national parks and reserves. The Great Victoria Desert Nature Reserve and the Nullarbor National Park are located in this region.

The Coastal Plains

The Coastal Plains of Australia stretch from Queensland to Victoria. This region is mostly a flat plain. The Coastal Plains form the eastern coast of Australia. This region is flat and low-lying. It is suitable for urban development. The largest cities—Sydney, Melbourne and Brisbane—are located along the coastal plains. The coastal plain is separated from the interior of the continent by mountains and the Great Dividing Range. This region is made up of the Brisbane River, parts of the Great Barrier Reef and many valleys and high rocky elevations.

Sydney

- The Great Barrier Reef is located off the northeastern coast of Australia. It is a complex system of coral reefs, shoals and islets lying in the Pacific Ocean. Coral reefs are diverse marine ecosystems that are built by colonies of tiny animals called corals. The Great Barrier Reef supports a diverse marine life which includes sea anemones, sponges, worms, lobsters, crayfish, prawns and crabs. Coral polyps are the key components of a coral barrier reef and it requires a stable climate. Therefore, climate change is perhaps the biggest threat to the Great Barrier Reef. Coral reefs flourish in clear, salty water that is low on phosphorous and nitrogen. The water of the sea is, however, getting polluted as the pollution from the land is entering the sea through the rivers and streams. Warm ocean temperatures put stress on the corals and lead to coral bleaching.

karst region: a landscape formed from the dissolution of soluble rocks such as limestone, dolomite, and gypsum; coral bleaching: when coral polyps expel algae that lives inside their tissues

Coral bleaching is a result of global warming and water pollution. Scientists believe that if the global temperature continues to increase in such an alarming manner, the coral polyps will not be able to recover from coral bleaching. Urban development along the coast has resulted in the loss of coastal wetlands which acted as a filter preventing acidic sediments and chemical run-off to enter the sea.

Australia is an island country lying between the Pacific Ocean and the Indian Ocean. You have learnt in this chapter that Australia has a low-lying landscape with wide stretches of desert. The interior of the continent is hot and dry and is also referred to as the outback. The northern part of the country experiences a tropical climate and receives heavy rainfall in the summer whereas the south experiences rainy winters. As it lies in the Southern Hemisphere, January and February are the hottest months whereas July is the coldest.

Most of the Australians live in the cities near to the sea and on the fertile south-east. Now you know why despite being an island, Australia gets the honour of being a continent. The varied geographical diversity, vast stretches of desert, amazing artesian wells and the natural wonders of the great Barrier Reef attract marine biologists, environmentalists, earth scientists and tourists to explore nature in all her glory.

The aborigines of Australia, being one of the most ancient tribes in the world, also attract anthropologists from around the world.

Geo Connect

Located in the north-east of North America, Greenland is the largest island in the world. It is located completely within the Frigid Zone. Covering an area of about 21.5 lakh sq. km., Greenland is separated from Northern Canada by the Baffin Bay and the Davis Strait. Nuuk is the capital of Greenland. Almost 80 per cent of the island is covered by snow and ice. Animals like reindeer, polar bear, musk ox and huskies can be found. All animals have thick fur to protect them from the extreme cold. The Inuits are the original inhabitants of Greenland.

In a Nutshell

- Australia is the smallest continent and is referred to as the island continent. It is located entirely in the Southern Hemisphere.
- Australia comprises six states namely, New South Wales, Victoria, Queensland, South Australia, Western Australia and Tasmania.
- The four main physical divisions of Australia are the Eastern Highlands, Central Lowlands, Western Plateau and the Coastal Plains.
- The continent has large stretches of desert with spectacular sand dunes.

Workout

A. Fill in the blanks.

1. Australia is located in the .... hemisphere.
2. .... is Australia's largest city.
3. .... is Australia's lowest region.
4. Coral .... are the key components of a coral barrier reef.
5. .... is an important lake in Australia

B. Fill in the blanks with the correct answers.

1. Australian native people are known as ....
   a. aborigines
   b. pigmies
   c. natives
   d. Inuit
2. .... is the capital of Queensland.
   a. Melbourne
   b. Sydney
   c. Brisbane
   d. Adelaide
3. Mt. Kosciusko is located in the ....
   a. Bass Strait
   b. Eastern Highlands
   c. Central Lowlands
   d. Great Dividing Range
4. .... is a saltwater lake in Australia.
   a. Lake Eyre
   b. Lake Alexandria
   c. Lake Victoria
   d. Lake Titicaca
5. The .... is the largest desert in Australia
   a. Sahara Desert
   b. Victoria Desert
   c. Thar Desert
   d. Kalahari Desert

C. Give one word for the following:

1. Smallest continent: ....
2. The longest river of Australia: ....
3. Australia's most important agricultural region: ....
4. Capital of New South Wales: ....
5. Van Diemen's land: ....

D. Give reasons.

1. Queensland is a popular tourist destination.
2. Climate change is harmful to the Great Barrier Reef.
3. Australia is called an island continent.
4. The Bass Strait is economically important to Australia.

E. Answer these questions in brief.

1. What do you mean by the following:

   a. Oceania b. Wren c. Cartons d. Aquifer e. Bass Strait

2. Name the political divisions of Australia.
3. How do the Eastern Highlands affect the climate of Australia?
4. What is the source of the Darling and the Murray rivers?
5. What are the indigenous people of Australia called?

F. Answer these questions in detail.

1. Write a short notes on:

   a. Victoria b. The Olgas

   c. Eastern Highlands in Australia d. South Australia

2. Based on the Western Plateau, answer the following:

   a. Where is the Western Plateau of Australia located?

   b. Write about the rocks found in this region.

   c. Is this region agriculturally productive? If not, why?

   d. Write about the Uluru that is found in this region.

3. Based on the great Barrier Reef, answer the following questions:

   a. Where is it located?

   b. What is the Great Barrier Reef? What is it made of?

   c. Why is it included in the seven natural wonders of the world?

   d. What type of flora and fauna is found in this region?

Think Box

The Great Artesian Basin is a spectacular feature of Australia. It is a large underground lake. The water from this lake comes out on its own and not by pumping. Find out the reasons for this.

Picture Study

Look at the picture and answer the questions.

1. Identify this structure.
2. Where is it located?
3. What is its significance?

Life Skills and Values

The native people of Australia are called the aborigines. They survive in the harsh climate of the sandy desert and the Western Plateau region. Discuss the importance of ethnic groups and their influence on culture, people and society. With the help of your history teacher, arrange a symposium on the topic 'Importance of ethnic groups in the modern society'.

Enjoy

Make a PowerPoint presentation on the Uluru and Olgas. Explain why is it one of the most remarkable geographical features of Australia.

Weblinks

For more information, visit
http://www.australia.gov.au/about-australia/our-country/the-australian-continent
Last accessed on 31/July/2020

14 Sheep Rearing in Australia

Let's learn about...

- conditions that support sheep farming in Australia.
- the development of sheep farming in Australia.
- the wool industry of Australia.

Key Terms

- sheep
- farming
- grasslands
- animal husbandry
- wool
- merino wool
- export
- Australia

Reflect

I give you fibre which keeps you warm in the severe winter months. You get me from a small animal called sheep. What am I? ....

It is believed that sheep were first domesticated in Central Asia. It was also a popular form of animal husbandry in Europe. However, the climatic conditions of countries outside Europe were more suitable for sheep rearing. Therefore, European settlers started practising sheep rearing in the countries located in the Southern Hemisphere. Australia was an ideal location for sheep rearing and gradually it became one of the biggest wool producers in the world.

Figure Out

What was the contribution of John Macarthur to the wool industry in Australia?

Merino was first introduced to Australia in the early nineteenth century. Australia accounts for about 70 per cent of the world's supply of merino wool which includes the softest and the finest varieties. Agriculture, especially that of wool, established Australia as a thriving economy with a substantial workforce, service industries and large port cites. Australian agriculture benefitted from many different agricultural practices, formal and informal land grants, overseas capital and access to

A merino ram

animal husbandry: a type of farming which involves taking care of animals to produce food; merino: a breed of sheep indigenous to Spain which yields high-quality wool

relatively cheap labour. Combined with invention, ingenuity and hard work, this has led to Australia becoming a leading exporter of fine wool, meats and grains. Australia was an export superpower of wool until the numbers came down in the 1960s because of the development of synthetic fibres. China is now the biggest importer of Australian wool in the world.

Conditions Favouring Sheep Rearing in Australia

Let us understand the geographical conditions which make Australia suitable for sheep rearing and the leading producer of wool.

Climate

Sheep rearing thrives well in the warm and dry climate of the temperate region. The sheep in the tropical regions produce short and coarse wool. Sheep rearing is mostly practised in regions with dry climate and less rainfall. However, plenty of drinking water is required for the sheep. Therefore, the dry climate of Australia is ideal for wool production though the temperatures are too high in the northern regions. In the drier regions, the sheep are mainly kept for wool whereas the sheep raised for meat are kept in the southeastern part of the country.

Pasture

Sheep rearing requires an adequate supply of grass. The quality and the yield of wool depends on the quality of the pasturage. Australia has a vast expanse of grassland vegetation which is suitable for rearing sheep. New South Wales and Victoria have the largest number of sheep rearing farms. The sheep here graze on ley and wheat stubble. The Merino sheep are kept on the relatively drier grasslands and scrublands of the hotter interior while the crossbred sheep are kept in the better watered and improved pastures.

FactPedia

The grasslands of Australia are called the downs. They form the pastoral and agricultural heart of Australia. These grasslands extend from southern Queensland through New South Wales and Victoria to southeast Australia.

Water

The availability of water is an important prerequisite for sheep farming. Australia has a few perennial sources of water. Therefore, sheep stations or farms are dependent on artesian wells. These are wells which have a natural flow of water. They are dug or drilled manually along their outcrops on the surface of the Earth. Sheep are small animals that can wander roughly about 5 km for water if they are to survive in the dry regions. Thus, the spacing of the sources of water determines the size and the grazing pattern of the flock.

Artesian well

pasturage: land covered with grass for animals to eat; ley: an area of land where grass is grown temporarily instead of crops; prerequisite: an important condition or a requirement

Green Earth

Australia experiences recurring droughts in the interior regions. Drought conditions make it difficult for the sheep to survive. It also keeps farmers from overstocking the flock. Inadequate rainfall causes a great loss to livestock. Thus, farmers have to refrain from overstocking.

DIY

The graph below shows the consumption of different types of fibres and wool. Look at the graph and answer the questions.

1. Which fibre is the most in demand product in the world?
2. Which fibre is least in demand in the world?

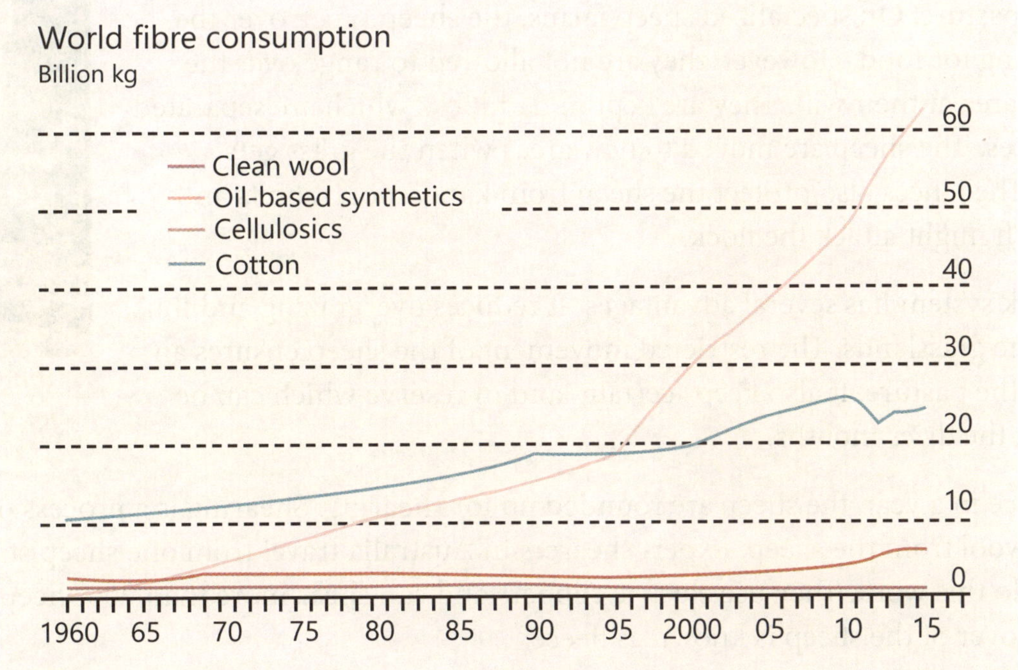

Accessibility

Apart from the climate and grasslands, Australian sheep farming farms also have the advantage of being near to the market. These farms are near big cities like Sydney and Melbourne. Australia exports ninety per cent of its wool production. The main market for the Australian wool is in Japan, the United Kingdom and many other European countries. Buyers from all over the world attend the major auctions. Australia has twelve wool marketing centres and it produces one-third of the world's total wool.

Wool production

A sheep farm

Mixed farming is dominant in Australia as compared to specialized wool production. This is because mixed farming is a steadier source of income for the farmers. However, in the interior regions of Australia, sheep farming is the principal agricultural activity.

Crossbred sheep account for one-third of the Australian flock. Selective breeding and better farming methods have greatly improved wool production. The supply of water to the pens and the cultivation of fodder producing crops have improved the quality and quantity of wool.

A dingo, a wild canine found in Australia

Sheep graze on natural grasslands. Thus, the pasture lands are improved by sowing clovers or grasses. Fertilizers are applied to promote growth of the natural pasture. On specialized sheep farms, the sheep range over the land searching for food. However, they are not allowed to range over the entire farm area at their will. They are kept in paddocks which are separated by wire fences. The sheep are moved to new areas when the grass gets exhausted. The fences also protect the sheep from kangaroos, rabbits and dingos which might attack the flock.

The paddock system has several advantages. It reduces overgrazing and thus, conserves the grasslands. The restricted movement of the sheep ensures an even use of the pasture. It also keeps certain land in reserve which can be used during the drier months.

Once or twice in a year, the sheep are rounded up for shearing. Shearing is a process of removing the hair or wool from the sheep. Expert shearers in Australia travel from one sheep station to another to do this work. They use electric clippers and can shear more than 200 sheep in a day. The soft wooly cover of the sheep is known as fleece.

Wool processing

Wool processing

Wool is usually transported and auctioned in the form of the grease (unprocessed wool) or as it comes from the animals. The first operation is the cleaning of the wool. The wool is combed in order to separate the fibres and then spun, woven and finished. There are basically two processes—producing either worsteds or woolens. Worsted is a particular way of spinning yarn and is made from long staple pasture wool. It is mainly used to make tailor garments.

fodder: food for farm animals; range: (of a person or animal) travel or wander over a wide area; paddocks: a field or plot of land enclosed by fencing or defined by natural boundaries

For making worsteds and woolens, it is necessary to dye the yarn before weaving it into different patterns of fabrics. The worsteds are tightly woven to produce smooth, high quality pattern cloth. Woolens are made from a much wider range of wool than worsteds and are more versatile. Some of the specialized woolen materials are serge, flannel and tweed.

Economic Importance of Sheep Farming

The sheep farming industry is the most iconic economic sector of the Australian economy. It is a major exporter and source of employment in Australia. Initially, this industry was concerned with wool production and later on meat. The huge bulk of the unprocessed wool which is referred to as greasy wool is exported and earns foreign exchange for the country.

You have already read about New South Wales and Victoria. These two states account for the largest share of the total value of the sheep farming industry.

The farmers of Australia are also taking simple steps to improve environmental sustainability. They install solar panels, fence off dams to increase the biodiversity of the area and take up different grazing strategies to improve soil health and ground cover. They also look after the welfare of the animals and ensure a sustainable supply of fodder.

Australia is the most important wool producer in the world. Sheep rearing is an important economic activity in Australia as it gains from the export of wool. You have read that the sheep kept primarily for wool thrive better in the drier areas. In these regions, the sheep farms are often very large as they have low vegetation cover. Sheep farms in these areas thus extend to several hundred sq. kilometers whereas in the wetter areas, the farms are smaller in size because the grass is more abundant and of better quality. Thus, it may be concluded that the sheep vary in size according to the available pasturage. The yield of wool also depends upon the quality of pasture.

Geo Connect

Argentina has the third largest sheep numbers in the world. Almost 75 per cent of the sheep in Patagonia, are Merino. Sheep farming has been the most important economic sector in the region since the 19th century. Wool sales represent up to 80 per cent of the total farm income. Today, sheep farmers have adopted sustainable methods like pasture rotation and grass farming to restore the grassland area.

In a Nutshell

- Australia is the leading producer of wool. It contributes to the economic growth of the country as it is mainly an export industry.
- The geographical setting of Australia, the climatic condition and the pasture land provide impetus to the growth of this industry.
- Sheep are reared mainly for wool and meat. Australian farmers also work on the animal welfare to main the sustainability of this industry.

Workout

A. Fill in the blanks.

1. Sheep was first domesticated in ....
2. Downs extend from .... to ....
3. Sheep are reared for .... and ....
4. The quality of yield of wool depends on ....

B. Fill in the blanks with the correct answers.

1. Sheep thrive well in .... type of climate.
   a. temperate b. tropical
   c. frigid d. humid
2. Sheep farming in mainly concentrated in the .... in Australia.
   a. Central Lowlands b. Eastern Highlands
   c. New South Wales d. Coastal Plains
3. Shearing is done ....
   a. three times in a year b. every week
   c. every day d. once or twice a year
4. .... are the main source of water to sheep cultivators.
   a. Perennial wells b. Perennial rivers
   c. Artesian wells d. Streams

C. Give one word for the following:

1. Clipping of wool from the bodies of the sheep ....
2. Animals from where wool is extracted ....
3. Unprocessed wool ....

D. Answer these questions in brief.

1. How does climate influence sheep farming?

2. What do you mean by the following terms:
   a. fleeces
   b. shearing
   c. worsted
   d. downs
3. What are paddocks? Why are they important in sheep farms?
4. Name some specialized woolen materials.

E. Answer these questions in detail.

1. Based on wool, answer the following questions:
   a. What is wool? From where do we obtain wool?
   b. Name the different varieties of wool available.
   c. Why is wool an important fibre?
2. How is wool processed?
3. Explain the economic importance of sheep farming in Australia.

F. Map Work

On an outline map of Australia, mark the following:

1. Downs
2. Two areas of sheep rearing
3. Sydney
4. Melbourne

Think Box

Sheep stations are large areas in Australia where the main activity is raising sheep for their wool and meat. Explain what impact severe drought might have on sheep rearing.

Picture Study

Look at the picture and answer the questions.

1. Explain the importance in sheep rearing.
2. What are sheep pastures known as in Australia?

Life Skills and Values

Animals play an important role in our life. We derive most of our needs from animals. Make a list of the ways by which we can protect and preserve them.

Enjoy

Discuss the importance of animal husbandry in the economy of a country. Organize a panel discussion and find out how animal husbandry leads to development in the rural areas of any country.

Weblinks

For more information, visit http://www.abs.gov.au/ausstats/abs@.nsf/featurearticlesbyCatalogue/1476D522EBE22464CA256CAE0015BAD4?OpenDocument
Last accessed on 31/July/2020

Across the Boundary 4

Be An Oceanographer

Imagine you are an oceanographer working to protect the beautiful, diverse underwater natural wonder that is the Great Barrier Reef. Develop a newsletter for the conservation of the reef. Work on the following points:

- Where is the reef located?
- What kind of marine life is found in the reef?
- What are the threats to the Great Barrier Reef?
- Why is the Great Barrier Reef important to the marine environment?
- What is the economic importance of the Great Barrier Reef?

1. With the help of your biology teacher, find out about the marine ecosystem prevailing in the Great Barrier Reef. Include different marine life thriving in the reef and find out how they are interdependent and interrelated to each other.
2. With the help of your geography teacher, find out about the climatic threat on the Great Barrier Reef. Also, analyze the human action which is major a threat to the reef.
3. Conclude the newsletter stating the economic and the environmental importance of corals in the Great Barrier Reef.

Snap Recap

Types of Rocks

- **Igneous Rocks**
  - formed by the cooling of molten magma
- **Sedimentary Rocks**
  - formed by transportation, accumulation and cementation
- **Metamorphic Rocks**
  - formed due to high temperature, pressure and chemical reaction

Soil Erosion

- **Running Water**
  - **Gully Erosion**
    - occurs on steep slopes devoid of natural vegetation, occurs mostly in hilly regions
  - **Sheet Erosion**
    - occurs on steep slopes devoid of natural vegetation, occurs mostly in hilly regions
- **Wind Action**
  - **Wind**
    - wind removes topsoil with no vegetation cover, occurs mostly in desert regions
- **Human action**
  - **Farming**
    - removing natural vegetation for farming increases soil erosion

Energy Resources

Conventional Sources

- **Coal** — causes a lot of air pollution, wide range of uses from domestic to commercial
- **Petroleum** — used as a lubricant for machinery, wide range of use from domestic to commercial
- **Natural Gas** — environment friendly, has a wide range of uses

Non-conventional Sources

- **Sun**
- **Wind** — the Sun, wind and tides create less pollution, rebewable sources of energy
- **Tides**
- **Nuclear Energy** — radioactive waste is very harmful for the environment

---

Physical Features of Europe

- **Northwestern Highlands** — located in Scandinavia and Scotland, consists of old fold mountains, coastline is irregular, fjords
- **Central Highlands** — located in South Central Highlands, young fold mountains, consists of active volcanoes, Mont Blanc is highest peak
- **Central Plains** — consist of plateaus; Meseta Central, Massif Central, Vosges, Ardennes, Bohemian Plateau
- **Alpine Mountain System** — stretchs from the Atlantic Coast in the west to the Ural Mountains in the east; Rhine, Danube, Don and Volga are major rivers

Antarctica

- **Human Population**
  - does not have any indigenous popultion; known as the 'land of scientists'
- **Geographical Facts**
  - lies in the Antarctic Ocean around the South Pole; seasons are opposite of the Northern Hemisphere
  - Geographical divisions – Eastern Antarctica, Western Antarctica, Transantractic Mountain Range
- **Climate**
  - lies in the Antarctic Ocean around the South Pole; seasons are opposite of the Northern Hemisphere
  - Geographical divisions – Eastern Antarctica, Western Antarctica, Transantractic Mountain Range
- **Vegetation**
  - cannot support most plant and animal life, mosses, algae and lichens grow in the summer season

---

Cocoa Cultivation in Ghana

- **Geographical Factors**
  - **Sunshine**
    - cannot tolerate direct sunlight, forest cover of Ghana provides right amount of sunlight
  - **Soil**
    - requires well-drained, deep, porous soil; lowlands of Ghana are suitable; needs large humus content
  - **Climate**
    - a tropical crop, requires high temperature and rainfall, Ghana is located in tropical region
- **Economic Factors**
  - **Proximity to Market**
    - accouts for 60% of Ghana's export, exported via sea routes
  - **Labour**
    - labour intensive, labour plays an important role in cultivation, harvesting and processing

Note for students: The Snap Recap section contains a collection of concept maps that draw the outline of the concepts of you have learned in this book. Mind mapping is a useful technique that helps you learn more effectively and improves the way that you record information. They help you see the way pieces of information fit together. Mind maps also help you remember information, as they hold it in a format that your mind finds easy to recall.

TEST YOURSELF I

Full Marks: 50

A. Fill in the blanks. 1×5=5

1. The boundary between the stratosphere and the troposphere is called the ....
2. The bottom of the exosphere is called the ....
3. Information such as major highways and human settlements are shown in .... colour.
4. The greater the pressure difference between two places, the .... the wind will move.
5. On a .... scale maps man-made features are not shown.

B. Fill in the blanks with correct answers. 1×5=5

1. The intersecting point where a tributary comes and joins the main river is called ....
   a. confluence b. meeting point c. waterfall d. tank
2. Numerical fraction scale is also known as ....
   a. verbal scale b. linear scale
   c. representative fraction d. graphical scale
3. The ozone layer in located in ....
   a. troposphere b. stratosphere c. mesosphere d. ionosphere
4. All cultivated land is shown with a shade of .... on the map.
   a. green b. blue c. white d. yellow
5. Vertical movement of air is called ....
   a. wind b. current c. waves d. jet stream
6. A wind coming from west to east is called ....
   a. westerly wind b. easterly wind
   c. northerly wind d. eastern wind
7. When temperature is high, the pressure is ....
   a. low b. high
   c. pressure does not depend on temperature d. remains the same

C. Name the following. 1×5=5

1. Symbols used to represent man-made and natural features on the map.
2. The boundary between stratosphere and troposphere
3. Components of radiation from the sun.

4. The elevation between two successive contours.
5. Greenhouse gas

D. Draw the symbols of the following (as seen in topographical maps). 2×4=8

1. Post office
2. Unlined well
3. Footpath
4. Metalled road
5. Waterfall

E. Write T for true and F for false. 1×4=4

1. Map is expressed as a ratio of the distance on the map to the actual distance on the ground. ☐
2. Waterfall and glaciers are forms of precipitation. ☐
3. Wind is the horizontal movement of air. ☐
4. Sand dunes are represented by brown colour on a map. ☐

F. Answer these questions. 2×2=4

1. Convert the following verbal statement to representative fraction 2
   a. Convert 2 cm to 4 km into representative fraction
2. Convert the representative fraction to verbal statement 2
   b. Express 1:30000 as a verbal statement

G. Differentiate between the following. 3×3=9

1. Solar insolation and terrestrial radiation
2. Troposphere and thermosphere
3. Absolute humidity and relative humidity

H. Picture Study 2×5=10

1. What do you see in this picture?
2. How does this affect the environment?
3. What are the reasons that cause this?
4. How does it affect human health?
5. How does it affect animal survival?

TEST YOURSELF II

Full Marks: 50

A. Fill in the blanks. 1×5=5

1. .... is also called a primary rock.
2. .... and .... use windmills in India.
3. .... is the smallest country in the world.
4. .... and .... are small-scale industries.
5. .... is the currency of Switzerland.

B. Fill in the blanks with the correct answers. 1×5=5

1. The removal of weathered materials by agents of gradation is called ....
   a. weathering b. erosion c. removal d. degradation
2. Slate is a kind of .... rock.
   a. igneous b. sedimentary c. metamorphic d. secondary
3. .... is known as the 'land of windmills'.
   a. India b. Finland c. Netherlands d. Germany
4. ....-based industry produces furniture.
   a. Forest b. Agro c. Marine d. Mineral
5. The .... separates Europe from Asia.
   a. Ural mountains b. Black sea c. Caspian Sea d. Isthmus of Panama

C. Name the following. 1×5=5

1. Highest mountain peak of the Swiss Alps ....
2. The accumulation of sediments and the subsequent transformation into rocks ....
3. Benelux nations ....
4. Sources of nuclear energy ....
5. Chain of young fold mountains in Europe ....

D. Write T for true and F for false. 1×5=5

1. Petroleum and paraffin wax are petroleum products. ☐
2. SAIL is a large scale industry. ☐
3. Zurich is the capital of Switzerland. ☐
4. Coal is a non-conventional energy source. ☐
5. The Ganga and the Yamuna are major rivers of Switzerland. ☐

E. Look at the picture and answer the questions. 5

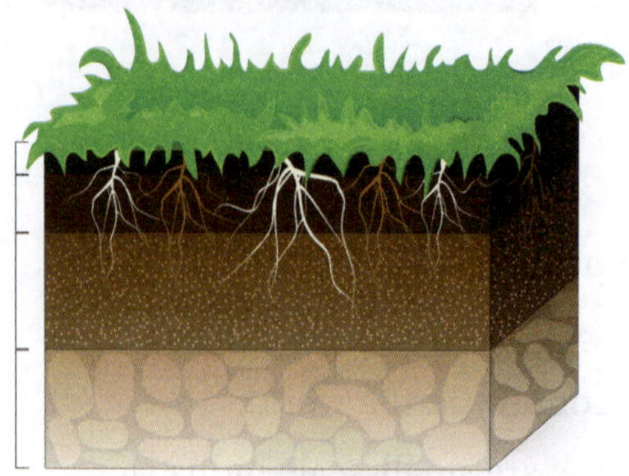

1. Label the diagram. 1/2×4=2
2. How is the above structure formed from rocks? Explain. 2
3. Give an example of soil formed in situ. 1

F. Thousands of people visit Switzerland every year. Based on this fact, answer these questions. 5

1. Where is this country located? 1
2. Why has this country developed as a popular tourist spot? 1×4=4

G. Give geographical reasons for the following. 2×3=6

1. Soil conservation is a matter of international concern.
2. Advancement of wind energy utilization will have a positive impact on the environment.
3. Labour availability is a necessary factor in determining the location of an industry.

H. Differentiate between. 2×4=8

1. Mechanical weathering and chemical weathering
2. Generation of thermal electricity and hydroelectricity.
3. Quartzite and flint
4. Large scale industry and small scale industry

I. On the outline of a map of Europe, mark the following places. 6

1. Lake Geneva
2. Highest mountain system in the Alpine Mountain System in Europe.
3. Italy's longest river
4. Zurich
5. Highest summit in Europe
6. The Ural Mountains

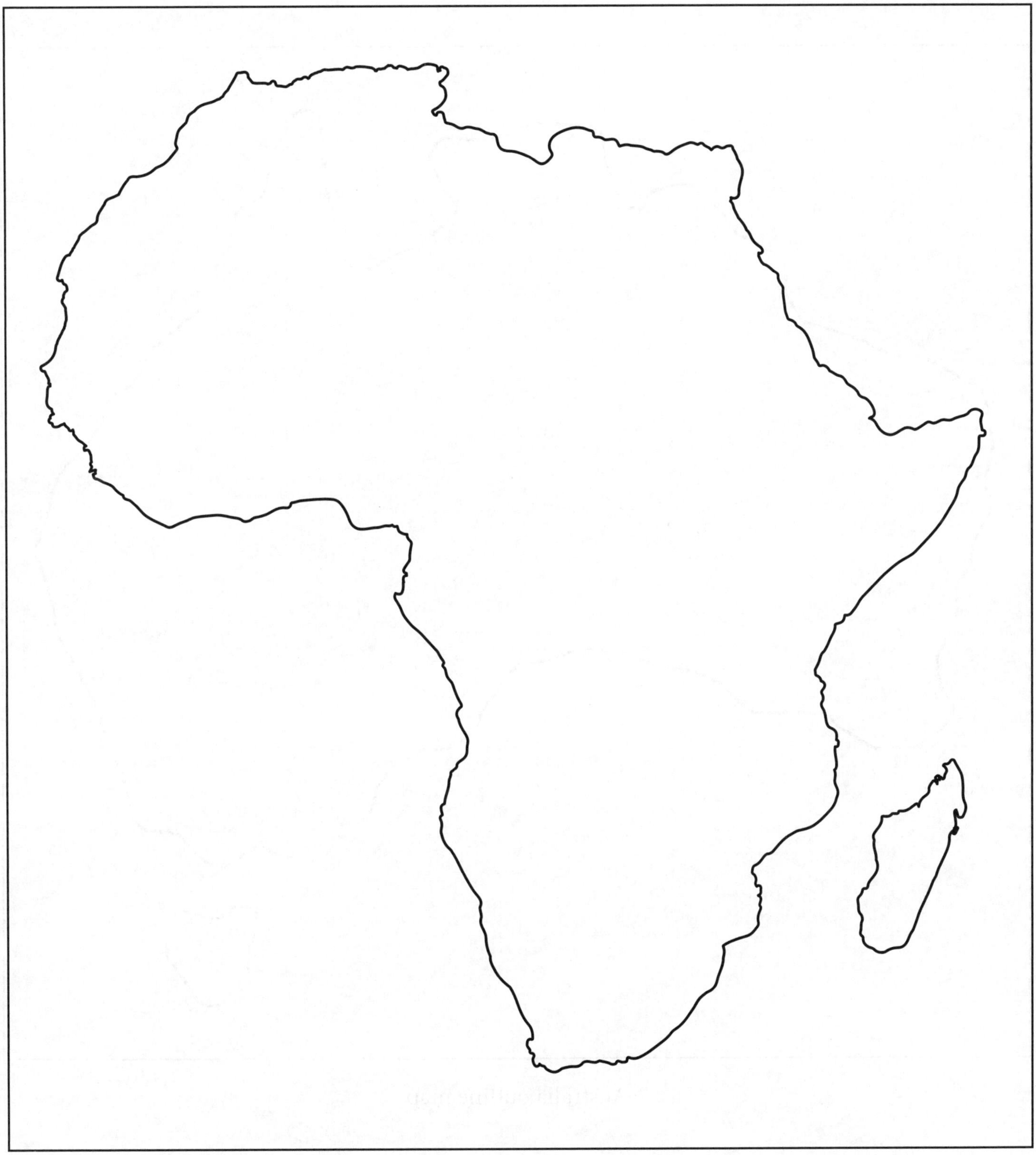

Africa outline map

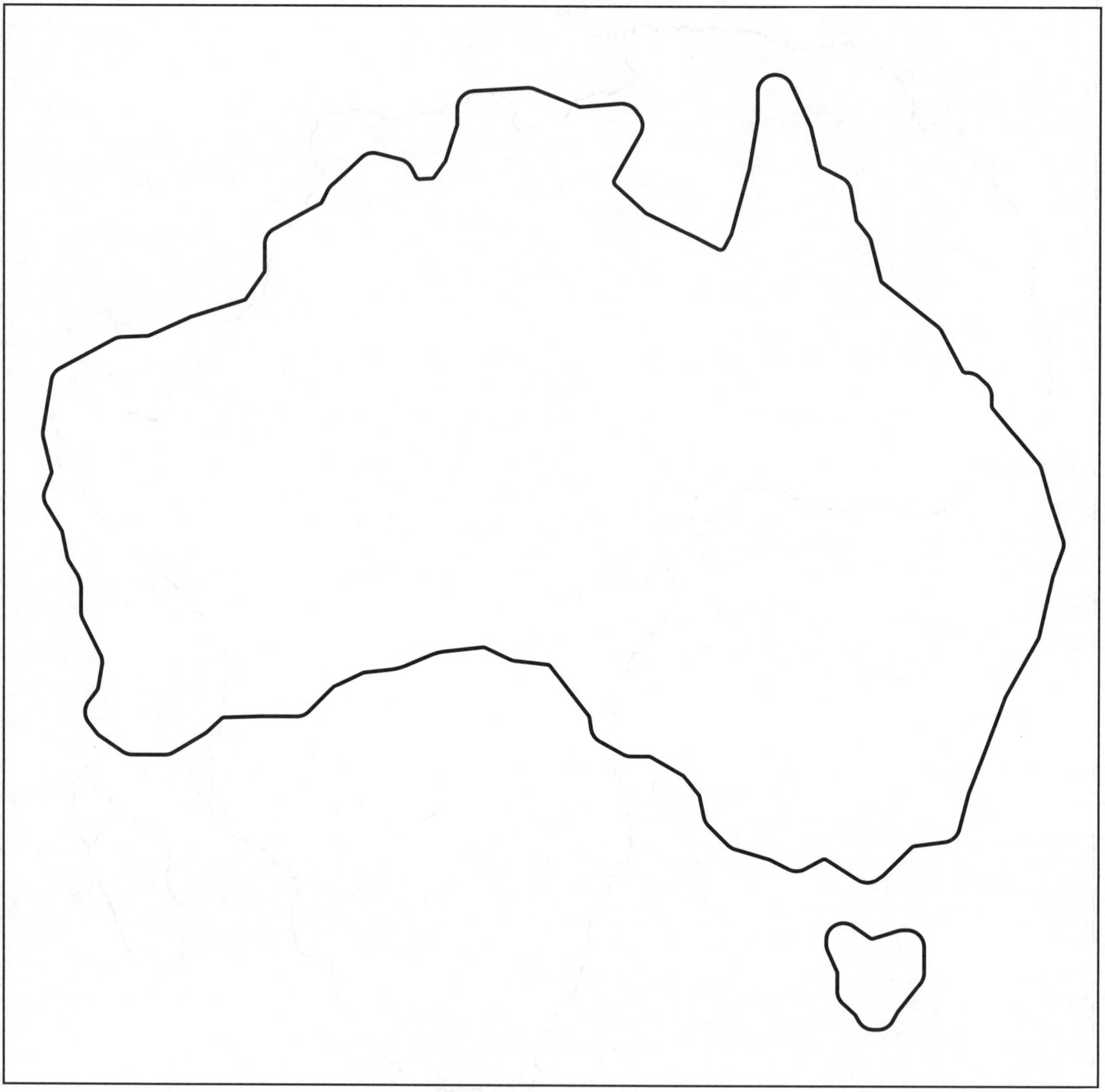

Australia outline map

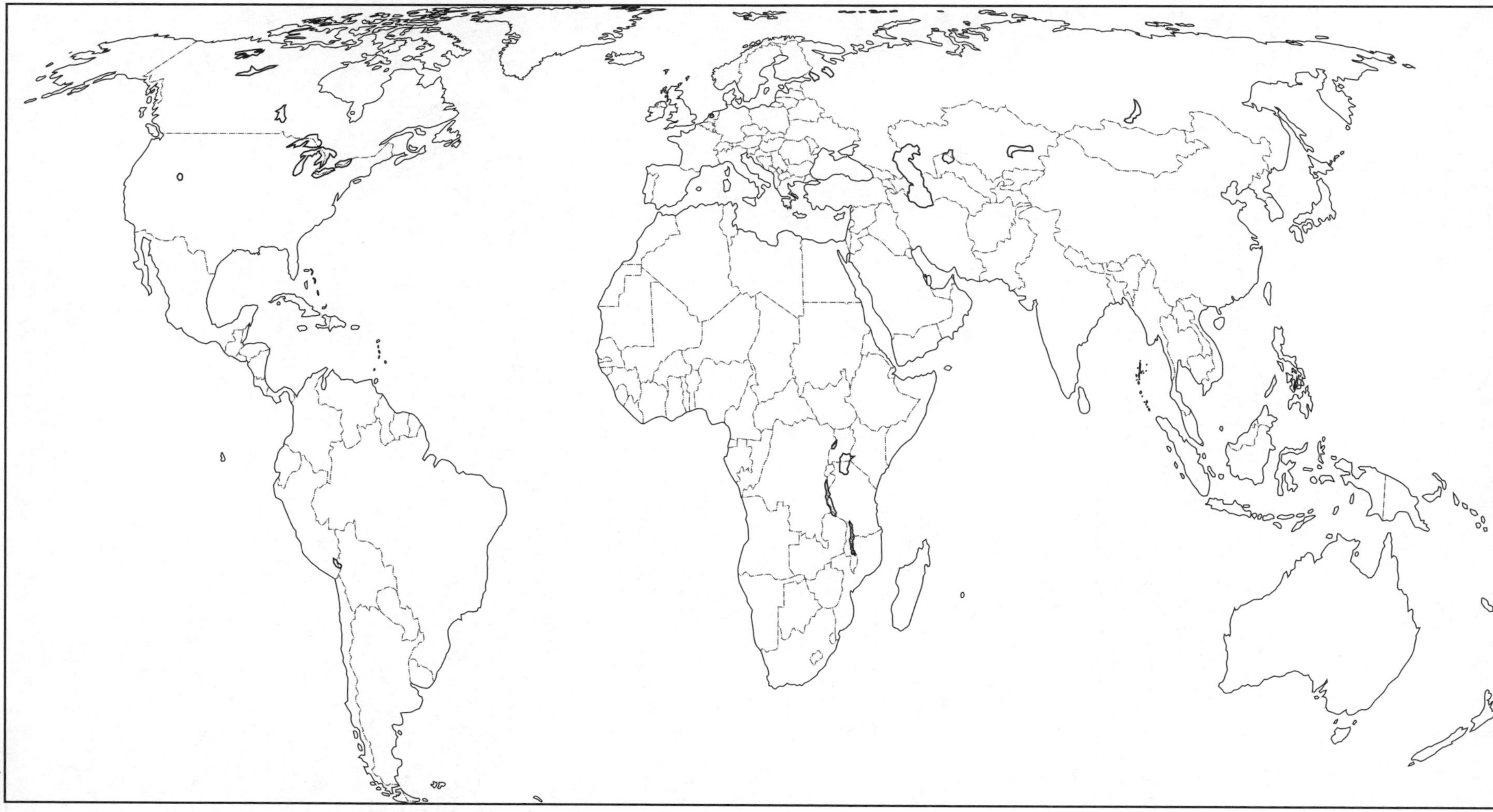

Political Map of World-Outline

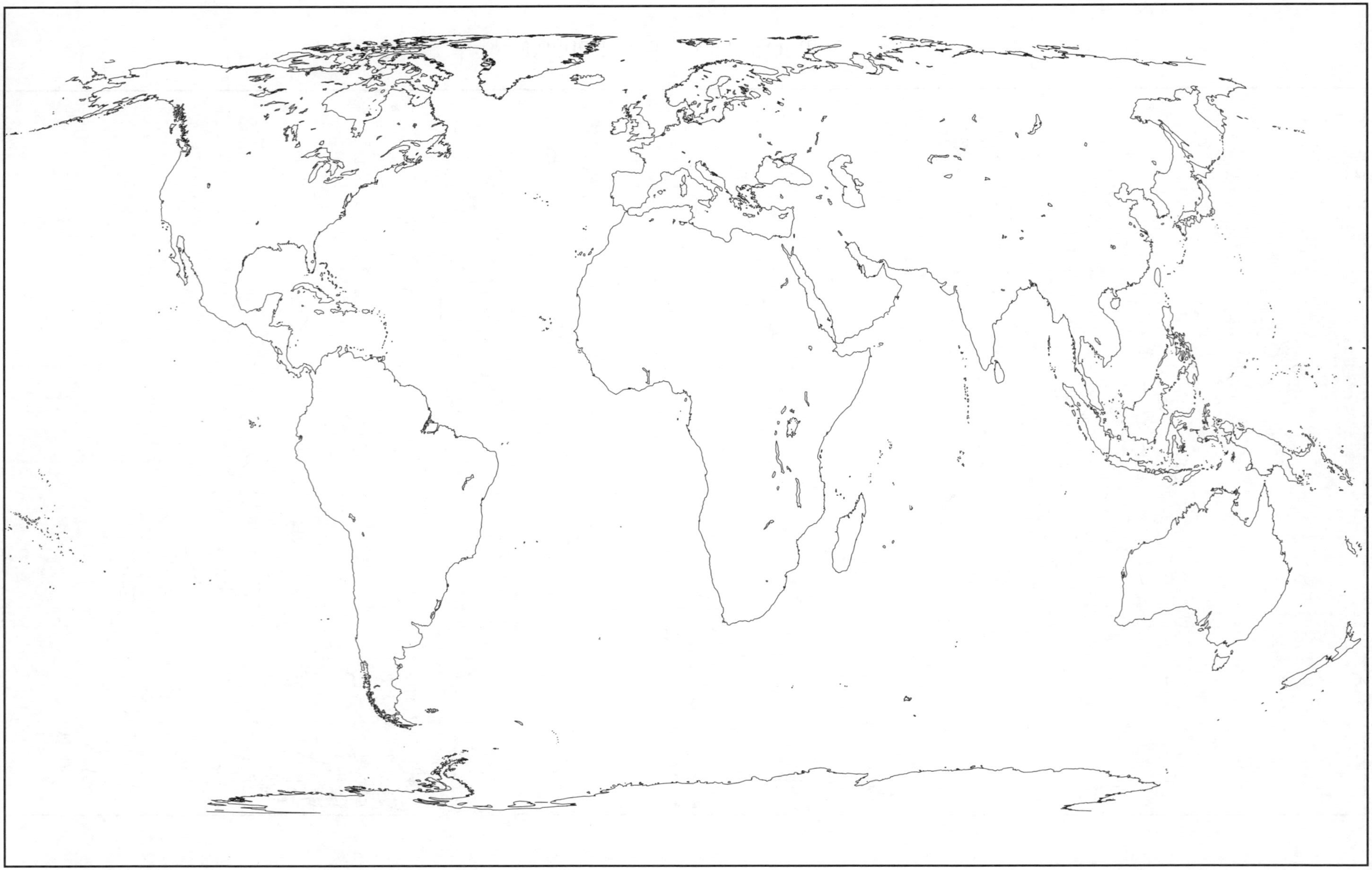

Physical Map of World-Outline